The Illustrated
Six Wives
of
Henry VIII

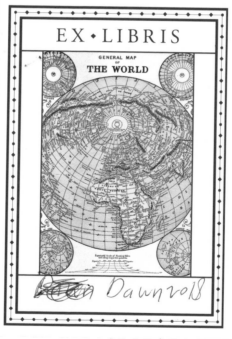

EX · LIBRIS

GENERAL MAP
OF
THE WORLD

AMBERLEY

First published 2015

Amberley Publishing
The Hill, Stroud
Gloucestershire, GL5 4EP

www.amberley-books.com

British Library Cataloguing in Publication Data.
A catalogue record for this book is available from the British Library.

ISBN 978 1 4456 4287 1 (paperback)
ISBN 978 1 4456 4300 7 (ebook)

Typesetting and Origination by Amberley Publishing.
Printed in Great Britain.

Contents

· ANNO · ETATIS · SVÆ · XLIX ·

The best-known portrayal of Henry VIII. (Library of Congress)

Introduction

The Six Wives of Henry VIII

Everyone knows the rhyme 'Divorced, Beheaded, Died, Divorced, Beheaded, Survived', which neatly sums up the fates of the six women unlucky enough to marry Henry VIII. Behind the stereotypes, however, were six very different individuals who were each, in their turn, queen of England.

Catherine of Aragon, Henry VIII's first wife, was married to him for nearly twenty-four years – far longer than his other five marriages combined. The Spanish princess, who was five years older than her husband, served as regent during the king's absence in France, and wielded real political power. She was eventually discarded due to the failure of her sons to survive, as well as Henry's desire to marry Anne Boleyn. Contrary to the rhyme, her marriage ended with an annulment rather than divorce, something which meant that it had been invalid from the start and that, legally, she had never been queen of England at all.

The 'beheading' of the second wife, Anne Boleyn, conceals a story of great passion, with Henry risking war and excommunication to marry the lowly daughter of a knight. Anne, although not beautiful, was fascinating, intelligent and charming. She was also the leader of her own political faction at court and a major patron of religious reform in England. Like her predecessor, she failed to give the king the heir he craved. Following the pattern of his first union, Henry's second marriage was also annulled. It must have been a bitter irony to Anne Boleyn that she was beheaded for adultery when, as far as the law was concerned, she had never truly been married.

Henry VIII's first valid marriage (as far as he was concerned), was to Jane Seymour. Jane, who was the lowest born of all the six wives, presented herself as meek and mild, but there are hints in the sources that she too was interested in political affairs. As a woman who was 'not very secure', she stayed quiet to ensure her survival. It was a tragedy for Jane that she died only twelve days after giving the king his longed-for son. If she had lived – as the mother of the Prince of Wales – she could never have been discarded.

The second 'divorce' of the rhyme was, in fact, a third annulment. Jane Seymour's sudden death left Henry without a candidate for his fourth wife. His initial attempts to obtain a French or Imperial bride proved fruitless with one potential wife, Christina of Denmark, declaring that 'if I had two heads, one should be at the King of England's disposal'. Instead, Henry turned to

Cleves, a semi-independent duchy in modern-day Germany, with links to the Protestant Schmalkaldic League. Unfortunately, Anne of Cleves proved to be a disappointment. While the king probably never declared that he had been sent a Flanders Mare instead of a woman, he was anxious to end the marriage. It was annulled after only six months.

Shortly after his third annulment, Henry married the young Catherine Howard, who was a first cousin of Anne Boleyn. Unlike her cousin, who was innocent of the charges of adultery, Catherine was probably guilty. She was certainly no virgin at the time of her marriage and, in February 1542, followed her cousin to the block. This fifth marriage was never annulled and so, technically, Catherine died a queen and as Henry's second lawful wife.

With the execution of Catherine Howard, few women were willing to risk marriage to Henry VIII and it took him a year to find a new bride. Catherine Parr had already been widowed twice and was in love with another man, but Henry was determined. She saw her elevation as a sign from God, but came close to arrest for heresy. Like her namesake, Catherine of Aragon, she was also called upon to act as regent. Catherine Parr took an interest in the royal children, helping to bring the king's two daughters back into the succession to the throne. Although the wife who 'survived', she did not do so for long, dying in childbed less than two years after her royal husband. Her fourth marriage, to Thomas Seymour, meant that the last wife of England's most married king was also the kingdom's most married queen.

Throughout his reign, Henry also took mistresses, with Mary Boleyn – Anne's sister – and Bessie Blount – the mother of his only acknowledged illegitimate child – the most prominent. At various times there were rumours that Bessie, or some of her successors to the king's bed, might also become his queen. Certainly, had he lived longer, a seventh wife is not unlikely.

No other English king has come close to Henry VIII's total of six marriages. The story still enthrals today, with the lives of the six queens among the most well-known of the early modern period.

Henry VIII, anonymous after Hans Holbein. (Rijksmuseum)

Arthur Tudor, Henry VIII's elder brother, the heir to the throne and Catherine of Aragon's first husband. His death in 1502 left Catherine of Aragon a widow and available to marry Henry. (David Baldwin)

Catherine of Aragon

Although remembered for his many wives, Henry VIII spent two thirds of his adult life married to just one woman – his first wife, Catherine of Aragon. It was Catherine who witnessed the young king's accession, his attempts to establish himself as a ruler and an international statesman. For Catherine, her husband was always the handsome young prince who had rescued her from miserable obscurity, but their marriage ended with bitterness and recriminations on both sides.

Catherine of Aragon (1485–1536) was one of the most high-born of any queen of England. She was the daughter of two sovereigns, Isabella, Queen of Castile, and Ferdinand, King of Aragon, and descended from most of the royal houses of Europe. She was the couple's youngest child and was born on 16 December 1485 while her mother, the redoubtable Isabella, was undertaking a military campaign in southern Spain. Catherine's sex was a disappointment to her parents: of the family's five children, only one was a son. In September 1496 Catherine's brother, Juan, died and his widow bore a stillborn son a few months later. The next heir, Catherine's eldest sister, Isabella, Queen of Portugal, passed away in childbed and her only child, Manuel, Prince of Portugal, died aged two. These disasters devastated Catherine's family and drove her mother to seek solace in the church. It was the second sister, Juana, who ultimately succeeded their parents, only to be declared insane and unfit to rule. Catherine cannot have realised that her mother's misfortunes in losing her children would be mirrored, even more unhappily, by herself.

At the age of three, Catherine was betrothed to Arthur, Prince of Wales, who was the eldest child of Henry VII and Elizabeth of York and the living symbol of the union between the warring houses of York and Lancaster. Although childhood betrothals often came to nothing, the match was an excellent one for the English prince, while Catherine's parents hoped for a new alliance with England. The princess spent her childhood preparing for her future as queen of England, including building up a tolerance to beer, since the water in her new country was not widely considered fit to drink. She was always addressed as Princess of Wales.

Catherine was particularly close to her mother, who, after so many losses, was unwilling to part with her. She finally left Granada on 21 May 1501

Great Tournament Roll of Westminster depicting the king taking part in a joust to celebrate the birth of his eldest son by Catherine of Aragon. Sadly, the prince lived only a few short weeks. (Elizabeth Norton)

and set out for England. The first part of her journey was overland across Spain and she made slow progress, only sailing in late September. She landed at Plymouth on 2 October 1501. The arrival of the daughter of the famous 'Catholic Kings of Spain' enhanced the prestige of the English royal house and Henry VII was determined to demonstrate to the world that his son was the equal of his Spanish bride. Catherine spent the days before her wedding in the company of Arthur's mother, Elizabeth of York, and his grandmother, Margaret Beaufort. On 14 November she was escorted along a six-foot-high wooden stage in St Paul's cathedral that had been erected for her marriage. Arthur was waiting for her there and, both clad in gleaming white, the teenagers were married. Catherine was taken to the Bishop's Palace by Arthur's younger brother, the ten-year-old Henry, Duke of York. The wedding was followed by great feasting and dancing and, that evening, the couple were ceremonially put to bed together naked.

Neither Catherine nor Arthur can have realised the importance that would later be attached to their wedding night. Catherine was fifteen and Arthur a year younger and both were considered ready to live together as husband and wife. George, Earl of Shrewsbury, who was present when Arthur was conducted to Catherine's bedchamber later testified that he had assumed that the marriage was consummated. Sir Anthony Willoughby, a friend of Arthur's also claimed that the prince called for him the morning after the wedding, saying, 'Willoughby, bring me a cup of ale, for I have been this night in the midst of Spain.' He later boasted to his friend that 'it is good pastime to have a wife', again implying that the couple had a sexual relationship. Catherine always swore that her first marriage remained unconsummated and, while it is possible that this was a lie, it seems unlikely given her deep religious faith. More likely, Arthur's comments were the boasts of an inexperienced youth who was aware of what had been expected of him on his wedding night.

Regardless of what happened on the wedding night, publicly Catherine and Arthur fulfilled their roles as Prince and Princess of Wales, and in December 1501 they travelled to Ludlow to rule their principality. In late March, both fell ill with the dangerous sweating sickness and, on 2 April 1502, Arthur died, leaving Catherine a widow at the age of sixteen. Catherine was too ill to attend Arthur's funeral but, as soon as she was well, she was brought to London and kept under observation until it was certain that she was not pregnant. Once this had been ascertained, Arthur's ten-year-old brother, Henry, was created Prince of Wales.

Catherine had been raised to become queen of England and Arthur's death threw her hopes into disarray. On her arrival in London she was installed in Durham House on the Strand while her future was decided. When word reached Spain of Arthur's death, Ferdinand and Isabella instructed their ambassador to seek the return of Catherine and her dowry. Such an outcome was not in the interests of either set of parents and the Spanish ambassador was instructed to discreetly suggest a marriage between Catherine and the new Prince of Wales. This solution suited Henry VII and, on 23 July 1503, Catherine's new betrothal was agreed. From a political perspective, the new match made perfect sense and there was a precedent in Catherine's own family as her sister Maria had married the widower of their eldest sister, Isabella. Personally, Catherine cannot have been entirely happy as Henry's youth meant that she would have to wait several years for marriage. More immediately, the marriage treaty also required that she renounce her widow's dower, forcing her to rely on the charity of Henry VII, or the generosity of her father.

The death of Isabella in October 1504 was a personal blow to Catherine and it had consequences for her own future prospects. Castile was the more powerful of the two kingdoms ruled by her parents and, on Isabella's death, it passed to Catherine's sister Juana and her husband, the Archduke Philip of Austria. Catherine was reduced to merely being the daughter of the King of Aragon. On 27 July 1505 Henry VII made his son secretly renounce his betrothal before the Bishop of Winchester. Catherine was unaware of this, but she did notice a change in the king's conduct towards her. Soon after Isabella's death, he stopped her allowance, arguing that it was her father's responsibility to provide for her. Ferdinand was just as determined that Catherine's upkeep was Henry's responsibility and, between 1502 and 1507 she received no money from either king. Her desperate letters to her father indicate the difficulties she was in, since she was unable to pay the wages for her household or buy clothes or food. In one letter, Catherine wrote:

Now I supplicate your highness, for the love of our Lord, that you consider that I am your daughter, and that after Him I have no other good nor remedy, except your highness; and how I am in debt in London, and this is not for extravagant things, nor yet by relieving my own [people], who greatly need it, but only for food; and how the king of England, my lord, will not cause them [the debts] to be satisfied, although I myself spoke to him, and all those of his council, and that with tears: but he said that he is not obliged to give me anything, and that even the food he gives me is of his goodwill; because your highness has not kept promise with him in the money of marriage portion. I told him that I believed that in time to come your highness would discharge it. He told me that that was yet to see, and that he did not know it. So that, my lord, I am in the greatest trouble and anguish in the world. On the one part, seeing all my people that they are ready to ask for alms; on the other, the debts which I have in London; on the other, about my own person, I have nothing for chemises; wherefore, by your highness' life, I have now sold some bracelets to get a dress of black velvet, for I was all but naked; for since I departed thence [from Spain] I have nothing except two new dresses, for till now those I brought from thence have lasted me, although now I have nothing but the dresses of brocade. On this account I supplicate your highness to command to remedy this, and that as quickly as may be; for certainly I shall not be able to live in this manner.

Catherine's complaints eventually had some effect and Ferdinand sent her the formal credentials to act as his ambassador in England. Catherine took this role seriously and had her own cipher for coded dispatches. Her new role improved her position somewhat and she was still acting in this capacity when Henry VII died on 21 April 1509.

Catherine cannot have been sorry to hear of the death of her father-in-law but she must have been amazed at just how suddenly her position in England improved. Her marriage to Prince Henry had originally been meant to take place when he turned fifteen, but this birthday had come and gone with no talk of a wedding and, at the time of his accession, Henry VIII was nearly eighteen years old. He had lived a secluded existence and was anxious to prove his maturity to the world. One way of demonstrating this was to marry and Catherine was a conveniently available princess. The couple knew each other well and Henry, who was always a romantic at heart, believed himself in love, seeing her as a princess in distress. Catherine cannot have believed her good fortune, as Henry was known as the most handsome man in Europe. According to the report of a Venetian diplomat who met the king in 1515, he was

The handsomest potentate I ever set eyes on; above the usual height, with an extremely fine calf to his leg, his complexion very fair and bright, with auburn hair combed straight and short, in the French fashion, and a round face so very beautiful, that it would become a pretty woman, his throat being rather long and thick.

KATHERINA VXOR HENRICI .. viii.

The young Catherine of Aragon. (Ripon Cathedral)

He was a fine physical specimen and they made a good-looking couple at their marriage at Greenwich on 11 June 1509. In spite of the five year age gap between them, the couple had a number of interests in common and, for Catherine, Henry was the love of her life. They were crowned together shortly after their marriage.

The early years of her marriage were the best years of Catherine's life. Both she and Henry took part in dancing and other entertainments, presiding over a glittering court. Henry loved to appear in Catherine's apartments in disguise, believing that she did not recognise him, a game with which the queen always played along. A particular highlight for Catherine was the meeting between Henry and Francis I of France outside Calais in 1521, which became known as the Field of the Cloth of Gold. This was one of the most splendid events of Henry's reign as both kings attempted to outdo each other in splendour. Catherine was a major participant, entertaining the French king on a number of occasions.

The early years of Catherine's queenship were not entirely given over to pleasures, since she was acutely aware of her duties as a princess of Spain. She always promoted her father's interests in England, a fact she set out in a letter to Ferdinand soon after her marriage. 'As to the king my lord, among the reasons that oblige me to love him much more than myself, the one most strong, although he is my husband, is his being the so true son of your highness, with desire of greater obedience, and love to serve you than ever son had to his father.' Catherine found her inexperienced husband easy to influence and, in the summer of 1512, Henry invaded Gascony jointly with Ferdinand. Catherine genuinely believed that an alliance with her father was in England's best interests, but Ferdinand proved an unreliable ally, using the English invasion as a pretext for him to occupy Navarre. The campaign of 1512 was a success from Ferdinand's point of view but, for the English, it was an unmitigated disaster.

In June 1513 Henry decided to mount a further campaign against France in person. Catherine accompanied Henry to Dover and he paid her the compliment of naming her as regent of England. Soon after Henry left, the Scots invaded northern England. Catherine was not the martial Isabella's daughter for nothing and she raised an army, travelling north as far as Buckingham before leaving the defence of England to her commanders. The queen had an anxious wait for news. She was jubilant when word reached her that her army had won a decisive victory at Flodden in which James IV of Scotland and much of his nobility were killed. She was proud of her triumph and sent the Scottish king's blood-stained coat to Henry in France writing further that 'I thought to send himself unto you, but our Englishmen's hearts would not suffer it'. Catherine's achievements rather overshadowed Henry's own mediocre French campaign.

As queen, Catherine knew that her main role was to provide Henry with an heir, leading to regular pregnancies during the early years of her marriage. She miscarried a daughter a few months after her wedding. This was a disappointment

Henry VII and
Henry VIII by
Holbein. Part
of a design for a
mural at Whitehall
showing Henry
VIII, his parents
and Jane Seymour.
(Elizabeth Norton)

Henry VIII, Renold Elstrack. (Yale Centre for British Art)

The young Mary I (b. 1516). (Elizabeth Norton)

Mary Tudor. (Ripon Cathedral)

Cardinal Wolsey.
(Jonathan Reeve,
JR1169b2p7 15001550)

but neither she nor Henry was unduly alarmed. The queen was soon pregnant again, bearing a son on New Year's Day 1511. Henry held a grand tournament in celebration, jousting under the name of Sir Loyal Heart with his and Catherine's initials entwined in his livery. The joy proved to be short lived, however, as, on 22 February 1511, the little prince died at Richmond, to the grief of both his parents. Catherine 'like a natural woman, made much lamentation', relying on her husband for comfort.

Although devastated, the couple believed that they would soon have more children. Catherine became pregnant again in early 1513, although, like her first, this pregnancy ended in miscarriage. In February 1515 she bore a second son at Greenwich, but he was either stillborn or died soon after birth. On 18 February 1516 both were overjoyed when Catherine bore a healthy daughter. While the sex of the child, whom they named Mary, was a disappointment, Henry saw her as the promise of healthy sons to follow. This was not to be and Catherine's last pregnancy ended with the birth on 18 November 1518 of a stillborn girl. Within a few years of Mary's birth, it was clear that she would be Catherine's only surviving child and she focussed on preparing her for her likely future as queen of England, commissioning a book on the education of girls by the Spanish scholar Luis Vives. Catherine, as the daughter of a female sovereign, was unconcerned by the prospect of Mary's accession but, for Henry, it was deeply worrying.

Like her mother, Catherine became increasingly religious, coming to be regarded as something of a living saint. A friend of her daughter's, Jane Dormer, would later recall that the queen

> Rose at mid-night to be present at the matins of the Religious. At five o'clock she made herself ready with what haste she might, saying that the time was lost which was spent in apparelling herself. Under her royal attire she did wear the habit of St Francis, having taken the profession of his Third Order. She fasted all Fridays and Saturdays and all the Eves of our Blessed Lady with bread and water.

By the mid-1520s Catherine was following a punishing daily regime of religious devotions and she and Henry had grown apart. She had always ignored Henry's infidelities, but in 1527 he began a relationship with one of her ladies, Anne Boleyn, which was to prove very different from any of his earlier affairs.

Anne, unlike Henry's earlier loves, refused to become the king's mistress, insisting on marriage. Henry was besotted with her and by spring 1527 the couple had vowed to marry. On 5 May 1527 Henry led Anne out as his dancing partner for the first time, a public statement of his relationship and, twelve days later, an ecclesiastical court opened to try the validity of his marriage. Henry argued that the marriage was invalid due to Catherine's earlier marriage to his brother. He was unable to keep the court secret and Catherine knew of it within hours. As Henry had feared, she appealed to her powerful nephew, the Holy Roman Emperor, Charles V, who was the son of her sister Juana, and asked him to alert the pope. On 16 June 1527 Charles, who was determined to uphold his aunt's honour, sacked Rome and imprisoned the pope, making it a virtual impossibility for Henry to obtain a divorce.

Catherine was devastated when, following the failure of the ecclesiastical hearing, Henry took her aside privately and informed her of his doubts about the marriage. She burst into tears, leaving the king to retreat impotently from the room. He continued to petition the pope and, with Anne Boleyn still in her household, it was a difficult time for Catherine. The sixteenth-century historian George Wyatt recorded a story that confirmed the rivalry between the two women:

> And in this entertainment of time they had a certain game that I cannot name then frequented, wherein dealing, the king and queen meeting they stopped, and the young lady's hap was much to stop at a king; which the queen noting, said to her playfellow, My lady Anne, you have good hap to stop at a king, but you are not like the others, you will have all or none.

Charles V in the manner of Jan Cornelisz Vermeyen, *c.* 1530. (Rijksmuseum)

Both Henry and Anne were determined to be rid of Catherine. In April 1528 the pope agreed to send a legate, Cardinal Campeggio, to England to hear the case. Henry and Anne were jubilant at the news, unaware that Campeggio had been given secret instructions to delay matters as much as possible to ensure that Catherine's nephew was not offended.

Campeggio made slow progress to England, only arriving in October 1528. He promptly took to his sick-bed where he remained until early 1529 when he finally set about trying to 'persuade the Queen to a Divorce; and dissuade the King from it, as having either way the end he proposed: yet he failed in both'. For the pope, the ideal solution was for Catherine to enter a nunnery, allowing her to retire with honour and the king to remarry. This solution did indeed have its merits since the queen could have lived in some comfort as an abbess. She would also have been able to safeguard the position of her daughter and it is likely that, had she agreed to retire, Henry would have confirmed Mary's legitimacy and her position as heir apparent. It was not, however, something that Catherine, who loved her husband, could contemplate, and she declared to Campeggio that she had no vocation for the religious life. The papal legate had no better luck with Henry, commenting that the king was so convinced of the invalidity of his marriage that 'if an angel was to descend from heaven he would not be able to persuade him to the contrary'.

Campeggio was left with no option but to try the matter, opening a legatine court at Blackfriars on 18 June 1529 with Cardinal Wolsey. When Catherine was called to speak, she walked to the king and knelt at his feet. She then made a direct appeal, begging her husband in broken English for justice. According to her contemporary George Cavendish in his *Life of Cardinal Wolsey*, Catherine pleaded that:

> I beseech you for all the love that hath been between us, and for the love of God, let me have justice and right, take of me some pity and compassion, for I am a poor woman and a stranger born out of your dominion. I have here no assured friends, and much less impartial counsel. I flee to you as to the head of justice within this realm. Alas! Sir, wherein have I offended you, or what occasion of displeasure have I deserved against your will and pleasure – now that you intend (as I perceive) to put me from you? I take God and all the world to witness that I have been to you a true, humble and obedient wife, ever comfortable to your will and pleasure, and never said or did anything to the contrary thereof, being always well pleased and contented with all things wherein you had any delight or dalliance, whether it were in little or much. I never grudged in word or countenance, or showed a visage or spark of discontent. I loved all those whom ye loved only for your sake whether I had cause or no, or whether they were my friends or enemies. This twenty years or more I have been your true wife and by me ye have had divers children, although it hath pleased God to call them out of this world, which hath been no default of me.

She continued, insisting that she had been a virgin at her second marriage, before abruptly leaving the hall. As calls were made for her to return, she refused, saying 'it makes no matter, for it is no impartial court for me therefore I will not tarry'. Catherine maintained her refusal to return to court throughout the duration of the hearing and insisted that only the pope had the power to hear her case. While the hearing continued, she was visited by Wolsey who asked to speak to her in private. Catherine, who hated the chief minister and believed that he was responsible for the divorce, ordered him to speak his business in front of her household. When he spoke in Latin, she stopped him, insisting that he speak in English so that everyone assembled could hear, something that he did not dare do. Finally, Campeggio, aware that he could delay no more, declared before a furious Henry that he could give no judgment and that he had to revoke the case to Rome.

Henry was furious at the failure of the Blackfriars trial and, while it was a victory for Catherine, it was a hollow one. Throughout the early years of the divorce, the couple had continued to live in the same household and Henry, on occasion, had continued to dine with his wife. She had also continued to make his shirts, something which had infuriated Anne Boleyn when she discovered it. On 11 July 1531 however, Henry and Anne rode away from Windsor, without saying goodbye to Catherine: she never saw him again. More cruelly, shortly afterwards she was instructed to separate from her daughter and the pair were kept apart until Catherine's death.

The grave of Catherine of Aragon in Peterborough Cathedral, then the Abbey Church. She was buried as Princess Dowager, but subsequent generations have recognised her status as queen. (Elizabeth Norton)

Following her separation from Henry, Catherine was ordered to go to the More, one of his smaller and more isolated palaces. She spent the remainder of her life in isolation, moving from one residence to another as her household was gradually reduced in size. At Easter 1533, she received a deputation headed by the dukes of Norfolk and Suffolk and other lords who informed her that Henry had married Anne Boleyn earlier in the year and that Catherine would now be known as Princess Dowager of Wales, the title she was entitled to as Arthur's widow. Anne was publicly proclaimed queen soon afterwards and, on 23 May, the new Archbishop of Canterbury, Thomas Cranmer, declared Catherine's second marriage invalid on the basis that her marriage to Arthur had been consummated. The former queen never accepted the sentence, angrily striking through references to her as Princess Dowager in official documents with her pen.

Catherine had been staying at the manor of Ampthill when she was informed of Cranmer's verdict on her marriage but, in July, she was ordered to move again, this time to Buckden, a property that was considerably more remote. Catherine and Mary enjoyed immense public support in England and Henry feared that they might mount a rebellion against him. Wherever Catherine travelled, she was greeted by cheering crowds and, by sending her to the damp and unhealthy Buckden, Henry hoped to keep her out of the public's mind. Both Henry and Anne were exasperated by Catherine's defiance and sought to break her spirit. In late 1532 Anne Boleyn demanded Catherine's jewels and, in anticipation of the birth of her own child in the summer of 1533, she also ordered that her predecessor hand over a christening gown that she had brought with her from Spain, something that the former queen indignantly refused to do.

Catherine's health was broken by the years of struggle and by her unsanitary living conditions and, by December 1535, she was gravely ill. One of Catherine's greatest friends during the years of the divorce was Eustace Chapuys, her nephew's ambassador. Henry, pleased to hear of Catherine's illness, granted the ambassador permission to visit her and he rushed to Kimbolton where he found her in bed. The former queen was glad to see him, permitting him to kiss her hand before thanking him for the trouble he had taken with her and for his visit since, 'if it pleased God to take her, it could be a consolation to her to die under my guidance and not unprepared, like a beast'. Chapuys, who was fond of Catherine, tried to give her hope, informing her falsely 'that the king was very sorry for her illness, and on this I begged her to take heart and get well, if for no other consideration, because the union and peace of Christendom depended upon her life'. The ambassador's visit did indeed rally Catherine's spirits and, after four days, he left, believing his master's aunt to be out of danger.

Catherine suffered a relapse on the night that Chapuys left. She had brought a number of high-born Spanish maids with her to England in 1501 and one of these, Maria de Salinas, had married an Englishman, becoming Lady

Sir Thomas Boleyn, Earl of Wiltshire and Ormonde. Drawing by Hans Holbein. (Jonathan Reeve, JR974b61p686 15001600)

Willoughby. When she heard that Catherine was dying she set out without permission for Kimbolton and forced her way into the house. She went straight to Catherine and it was in her friend's arms that the former queen died on 7 January 1536 at the age of fifty.

Before she died, Catherine dictated one last letter to Henry, addressing him as 'My most dear lord, king and husband' before setting out her continuing love for him:

The hour of my death now drawing on, the tender love I owe you forceth me, my case being such, to commend myself to you, and to put you in remembrance with a few words of the health and safeguard of your soul which you ought to prefer before all worldly matters, and before the care and pampering of your body, for the which you have cast me into many calamities and yourself into many troubles. For my part, I pardon you everything, and I wish to devoutly pray to God that He will pardon you also. For the rest, I commend unto you our daughter Mary, beseeching you to be a good father unto her, as I have heretofore desired. I entreat you also, on behalf of my maids, to give them marriage portions, which is not much, they being but three. For all my other servants I solicit the wages due them, and a year more, lest they be unprovided for. Lastly, I make this vow, that mine eyes desire you above all things.

Far from grieving for his first wife, Henry celebrated Catherine's death by wearing yellow and, on hearing the news, exclaimed, 'God be praised that we are free from all suspicion of war.' When Catherine's body was examined her organs were all found to be healthy save her heart, to which a black mass was attached. This immediately gave rise to suspicions that the queen had been poisoned and, while this had no basis in fact, the prime suspect was her rival, Anne Boleyn.

Henry VIII, Sylvester van Parijs. (Rijksmuseum)

Anne Boleyn

Anne Boleyn (*c.* 1501–36), the second and most famous of Henry VIII's wives, was not born to be a queen. Her date of birth was not recorded but it was most likely 1501. She was the second of the three surviving children of Sir Thomas Boleyn and his wife, Elizabeth Howard, and spent her childhood at Blickling Hall in Norfolk and Hever Castle in Kent. Although not royal by birth, Anne was far from lowly. Her mother was the daughter of the 2nd Duke of Norfolk and her father, while less well born, was the grandson of the Earl of Ormond. With the exception of her first cousin, Catherine Howard, Anne was the most nobly born of Henry's English wives.

Anne's father, Thomas Boleyn, was an ambitious man. He was the best French speaker at the English court and, in 1512, was sent as ambassador to Margaret of Austria, the regent of the Netherlands, in Brussels. The pair soon became friends and, by the time he returned home, Thomas had secured Margaret's promise of a place in her household for one of his daughters. Anne took up her prestigious post in 1513 and set about learning French, making an excellent impression on the regent, who wrote to Thomas saying that she found his daughter 'so pleasing in her youthful age'. When Anne arrived in Brussels, England was allied with Margaret and her father, the Emperor Maximillian. In August 1514, this friendship foundered and Henry VIII turned instead to Louis XII of France, arranging for his sister, Mary, to marry the elderly French king. Mary required Englishwomen to serve her and Thomas Boleyn secured a place for his eldest daughter, Mary Boleyn, in the French queen's household. Anne's presence was also required and she travelled from Brussels to France to join the new queen's household. Mary Tudor's time as queen of France was brief as her husband died, on 1 January 1515, after only a few short months of marriage. Anne then transferred to the household of Claude, the new queen of France.

Anne developed a love for her new home and she became French in all but birth, appearing exotic when she returned to England in 1522. It was not her choice to come home and she would probably have been happy to remain in France. However, in 1515, her great-grandfather Thomas Butler, Earl of Ormond, died. The earl had no sons and expressed the wish that Thomas Boleyn, his favourite grandson, should succeed him. In spite of this, the earldom was seized by his cousin, the powerful Irish nobleman Piers Butler, whom the English were loath to offend.

Thomas Boleyn appealed to the king and the dispute dragged on for some time. In 1522, the Earl of Surrey, who was the king's lieutenant in Ireland, suggested that Piers Butler retain the title and his eldest son, James, marry Thomas's only unmarried daughter. As a result of this, Anne was recalled and took up a position in Queen Catherine's household while the marriage was negotiated.

The Butler marriage was a neat solution to the problem of the Ormond inheritance, but Anne was not entirely happy with the match and looked around for something better. She was never described as a beauty. Her sixteenth-century biographer George Wyatt admitted that 'in beauty she was to many inferior, but for behaviour manners, attire and tongue she excelled them all. For she had been brought up in France.' Anne did not conform to contemporary ideals of beauty (blond hair and blue eyes), having instead dark hair and eyes. Claims that she had a sixth finger on one hand were greatly exaggerated, although George Wyatt had heard that she had a small extra nail on the tip of one of her fingers. It was a simple enough matter to hide this beneath fashionable hanging sleeves 'without any least blemish to it'. The defect was, however, well known enough at court for Catherine of Aragon to insist that Anne join her at cards regularly during the years of the divorce – ensuring that her extra nail was on display.

Anne Boleyn. (Ripon Cathedral)

Anne's wit, grace and poise more than made up for her lack of conventional beauty. Soon after her return from France, she was among the ladies who portrayed the seven virtues at a masque at Greenwich, dancing alongside the king's sister, who portrayed 'Beauty'. Anne, appropriately enough as it would transpire, acted the part of 'Perseverance'. Within months of arriving at court she had also attracted the interest of Henry Percy, heir to the earldom of Northumberland, who was a similar age to her and highly eligible. This was an excellent prospect for Anne and, according to her contemporary, George Cavendish, 'there grew such a secret love between them that at length they were engaged together, intending to marry'. Although both would later deny any promise to marry, they may well have come to an agreement. It was the loss of Percy that led to Anne's enmity towards Cardinal Wolsey. When the cardinal discovered the betrothal, he summoned Percy's father who indignantly removed his son from court and married him to a more suitable bride. Anne was sent home in disgrace.

Anne returned to court in late 1525 or early 1526 and once again took up a position in the queen's household. During her time at Hever, she may have become acquainted with a Kentish neighbour, Thomas Wyatt. They certainly enjoyed a flirtation following her return to court. Anne features in a number of Wyatt's poems as 'Brunet'. It was through Wyatt that Anne came to the attention of the king, with the pair vying for her attention until the poet eventually admitted defeat. It was a contest that he was never likely to win, as the married Wyatt knew well, reflecting in one of his verses:

> Whoso list to hunt: I know where is an hind
> But as for me, alas I may no more
> The vain trevail hath wearied me so sore,
> I am of them that farthest come behind
> Yet may I by no means be wearied mind
> Draw from the deer, but as she fleeth afore
> Fainting I follow. I leave off therefore,
> Sithens in a net I seek to hold the wind
> Who list her hunt, I put him out of doubt,
> As well as I may spend his time in vain,
> And graven with diamonds in letters plain
> There is written her fair neck round about
> 'Noli me tangere, for Caesar's I am,
> And wild for to hold, though I seem tame'.

He also, accurately, called Anne 'her that did set our country in a roar'. The king first noticed Anne through his friendship with Wyatt, with the pair's rivalry coming to the fore during a game of bowls. Henry, who had taken one of Anne's rings as a love token, used the finger on which he wore the jewel to point to the bowls, declaring, 'Wyatt, I tell thee, it is mine.' Wyatt, recognising this for the challenge it

[handwritten letter in early 16th-century secretary hand]

From Mrs Anne Bullen before her Maradg to the King:

ỹo humble and
obedyent ſervant

anne boleyn

A very flattering letter from Anne Boleyn to Cardinal Wolsey, written before her marriage. Anne thanks Wolsey for his help and promises that she will repay him if he manages to bring about her greatest wish of marriage to Henry. (Jonathan Reeve, JRCD3b20p899 15001550)

Letter from Anne Boleyn to Stephen Gardiner, the king's secretary, 4 April 1529. Anne was writing from Greenwich while Gardiner was in Italy for the second time petitioning for papal assent to Henry's divorce. (Jonathan Reeve, JR964b20p900 15001600)

Wolsey in his last days at Leicester Abbey, 1530. (Jonathan Reeve, JR1094b20fp904 15001550)

was, took out his own jewel, which he wore around his neck and asked for leave to measure the game, saying 'I hope it will be mine'. On recognising Anne's token, the king broke up the game and stalked away. Henry, at first, looked upon her only as a potential mistress but Anne, who had witnessed her own sister being discarded after several years in the king's bed, refused to countenance such a suggestion.

A number of Henry's letters to Anne survive. In 1526 Henry VIII was in his mid-thirties and, while not the handsome youth he had been, was still close to his prime. He was unused to a woman refusing him and, as the months passed and Anne continued to elude him, he became increasingly besotted. One letter, from early in their relationship, shows something of the depth of his feelings:

> For although by absence we are parted it nevertheless keeps its fervency, at least in my case and hoping the like of yours; assuring you that for myself the pang of absence is already too great, and when I think of the increase of what I must needs suffer it would be well nigh intolerable but for my firm hope in your unchangeable affection; and sometimes to put you to mind of this, and seeing that in person I cannot be with you, I send you now something most nearly pertaining thereto that is at present possible to send, that is to say, my picture set in a bracelet with the whole device which you already know; wishing myself in their place where it shall please you.

Anne continued to be unresponsive to the king's pleas to consummate their relationship. Finally, he came up with a radical solution, offering her the role of his official mistress and 'casting off all others than yourself out of mind and affection, and to serve you only'. This was a unique offer and is a testament to Henry's devotion, but Anne still refused. Finally, desperate, the king offered her the only thing that she would accept and, by spring 1527, the couple had decided to marry. To signify her acceptance – and the turmoil that she felt – Anne sent the king a gift of a jewel in the shape of a maiden in a storm-tossed ship.

An early letter from Anne to Henry survives which suggests that she returned at least some of the king's feelings, declaring, 'The joy that I feel in being loved by a king whom I adore, and to whom I would with pleasure make a sacrifice of my heart, if fortune had rendered it worthy of being offered to him, will ever be infinitely greater.' Henry's love for Anne Boleyn was the most passionate of his life and, once the couple had decided to marry, he began his long struggle to divorce Catherine of Aragon.

The long years of the divorce were particularly trying for Anne, who received much of the blame from contemporaries. She had a fiery temper and frequently quarrelled with Henry or made verbal attacks against Catherine of Aragon. Anne's main ire was reserved for Cardinal Wolsey, who had been her enemy since the loss of Henry Percy. When he first decided to divorce Catherine, Henry trusted Wolsey to arrange matters for him and Anne was prepared to work with the cardinal if he could secure her desires. After the failure of the trial at Blackfriars to end the marriage, Anne turned on the cardinal, intent on securing his ruin. According to George Cavendish, who was a member of Wolsey's household, Wolsey nicknamed Anne the 'Night Crow' and referred to her as a 'serpentine enemy' whispering in the ear of the king. Following the Blackfriars debacle, this enmity finally came out into the open with Anne writing to Wolsey, all pretence of friendship gone:

> Though you are a man of great understanding, you cannot avoid being censured by everybody for having drawn on yourself the hatred of a king who had raised you to the highest degree to which the greatest ambition of a man seeking his fortune can aspire. I cannot comprehend, and the king still less, how your reverent lordship, having allured us by so many fine promises about divorce, can have repented of your purpose, and how you could have done what you have, in order to hinder the consummation of it. What, then, is your mode of proceeding? You quarrelled with the queen to favour me at the time when I was less advanced in the king's good graces, and after having therein given me the strongest marks of your affection, your lordship abandons my interests to embrace those of the queen. I acknowledge that I have put much confidence in your professions and promises, in which I find myself deceived. But, in future, I shall rely on nothing but the protection of Heaven and the love of my dear king, which alone will be able to set right again those plans which you have broken and spoiled, and to place me in that happy station which God wills, the king so much wishes, and which will be entirely to the advantage of the kingdom.

Anne was determined to bring Wolsey down and she used her influence with Henry to turn his doubts about the cardinal's loyalty into hatred. Finally, in October 1529, Henry charged the cardinal with taking orders from the pope and brought about his ruin. The following year Anne secured her final revenge, arranging for Henry Percy to arrest Wolsey and bring him to London for trial. Wolsey died a broken man during the journey.

Once it became clear that there would be no papal annulment, the couple looked for a more radical solution and it was Anne who first suggested the possibility of breaking with Rome. She was a great patron of religious reform and this solution appealed to her. In 1531 Henry declared himself Supreme Head of the Church of England, although the decisive break with the pope had still not occurred. In August 1532 William Warham, the aged and conservative Archbishop of Canterbury, finally died. This allowed the appointment of Thomas Cranmer, a Boleyn-family chaplain and a man who shared their reformist views. By the end of 1532, when it was clear that Anne, who had already been created Lady Marquis of Pembroke, would soon be queen, she and Henry consummated their relationship. They married secretly on 25 January 1533 when Anne was already in the early stages of pregnancy and, at Easter, she was acknowledged as queen. Her coronation followed in the summer.

Thomas Cranmer by Gerlach Flicke. Cranmer annulled Henry's first marriage and authorised his marriage to Anne. He also stood as Elizabeth's godfather at her christening on 10 September 1533. (Elizabeth Norton)

Anne adopted the motto 'The Most Happy' to signify her joy to the world. The couple were confident that their child would be Henry's longed-for son and it was with disappointment that they greeted the birth of their daughter, Elizabeth, on 7 September 1533. The princess was immediately declared heir to the throne and her parents were confident that she would soon be followed by brothers. The queen proved to be a fond mother to her daughter and, while Elizabeth was given her own household in her infancy, Anne visited her regularly and supervised her upbringing and welfare. She was ambitious for the pretty, red-haired child and, according to her chaplain, William Latymer, was anxious for Elizabeth to learn Latin, Hebrew, Greek, Italian, Spanish and French.

The birth of her daughter made Anne fiercely protective, bringing out a less attractive side of her character in her conduct towards Henry's elder daughter, Mary, who had been declared illegitimate and disinherited. She publicly declared of the teenager that she 'intended to bring down the pride of this unbridled Spanish blood', as well as stating that both Mary and her mother were 'rebels and traitoresses deserving death'. She also, at times, made more positive overtures to the girl, offering to exempt her from the menial task of carrying the tail of her gown at court if she submitted. To Anne – and to Henry – Mary was an obstinate child. As the king's disinherited elder daughter she was also a threat to Anne's own child, something which inspired the queen's attempts to bring about her stepdaughter's capitulation. She was also very popular, while Anne was not: one woman was arrested after reports were made that she had called the new queen a 'goggle-eyed whore'. There were also reports that the crowds who came to watch Anne's coronation procession cried out mockingly, 'HA! HA!' at the sight of the royal couple's entwined initials on their banners.

As queen, Anne continued to promote religious reform, particularly in relation to the publication of the scriptures in the vernacular. She kept a copy of the Bible in English on a desk in her apartments from which anyone was permitted to read. The queen would, on occasion, read from this common desk, as well as owning a copy of the Bible in French for her own personal use. As part of her interest in religious reform, Anne also sent commissioners to Hailes Abbey to investigate their famous relic of the blood of Christ. When she was informed that it was a fraud – either duck's blood or red wax – she went immediately to Henry to request that it be removed. As was expected of a queen, she was also charitable, distributing alms when she travelled and also paying to maintain scholars at Cambridge University. She took a personal interest in these scholars, writing to the Abbot of St Mary's that she had arranged for a monk, John Eldmer, to 'apply and continue his study and learning at my lord's university of Cambridge for the increase of virtue and learning'. She was far from pleased when the abbot attempted to thwart her in this, threatening him by letter that he should either immediately release Eldmer to his studies 'or else to signify to us in writing, by this bearer, a cause reasonable why you defer to accomplish our said request'. Anne was not a woman to cross. Another beneficiary of her largess was a Dr Crome, on whom she bestowed the parsonage of Aldermany in London. When Crome proved less than keen to take up this post, he received a letter from the queen commanding him to go since 'our express mind and pleasure is that you shall use no farther delays in this matter'.

Although Henry VIII had gone to extreme lengths to make Anne his wife, their marriage proved to be troubled. Only a few months after their wedding, the couple quarrelled when Henry took a mistress during Anne's pregnancy. In early 1534 Anne was once again pregnant and, on discovering that Henry had taken a new lover, she railed against him. She was horrified when her husband replied that 'she had good reason to be content with what he had done for her, which he would not do now if the thing were to begin and that she should consider from what she had come'. Anne was forced to hold her tongue and, in the summer of 1534, she miscarried. It took her until the end of 1535 to conceive again, but on the very day of Catherine of Aragon's funeral, in January 1536, she miscarried a son. Anne blamed the loss both on her fright at the news that Henry had fallen from his horse and the shock of seeing the king with a new love, Jane Seymour. When confronted, Henry stalked out of the room, muttering that 'he would have no more boys by her'.

Elizabeth I at prayer, from the frontispiece of *Christian Prayers and Meditations* (London: John Day, 1569), a multilingual prayer book that included many prayers reputedly composed by Elizabeth herself. (Jonathan Reeve, JR1168b4fp747 15501600)

Elizabeth I. (Jonathan Reeve, JR1114b66pviii 15501600)

Without a son, Anne was as vulnerable as Catherine of Aragon had been and she had made many enemies. One of her maids, Jane Seymour, had caught Henry's eye and, by spring 1536, he was considering marrying her. Jane was an ally of Princess Mary, who gave her support to Anne's rival. Even more dangerously, in early 1536, the queen quarrelled with the king's chief minister, Thomas Cromwell, and threatened that she would have him executed. This was enough for Cromwell to join with the other parties seeking Anne's ruin.

It would have been impossible for Anne's enemies to act without the king's consent, but he was eager to rid himself of the wife who he felt had promised so much and delivered so little. For Anne, the end came quickly. On 30 April 1536 Mark Smeaton, a young musician in her household, was arrested by Cromwell and tortured. By the following morning, he had confessed to committing adultery with the queen. On 1 May, the royal couple attended a tournament at Greenwich. During the jousting, Henry suddenly rose to his feet and, without saying a word, rode to Westminster with only six attendants. On the journey, he repeatedly questioned Henry Norris, one of his attendants, on his relationship with Anne. According to Norris's servant George Constantyne the king 'promised him his pardon in case he would utter the truth. But whatsoever could be said or done, Mr Norris wold confess nothing to the King, whereupon he was committed to the Tower in the morning'.

Anne Boleyn. (Elizabeth Norton)

Early on 2 May, several members of the king's council came to arrest Anne at Greenwich. After interrogating her, she was taken to the Tower by water, a place from which she would never emerge. Anne, who was usually so composed, was terrified and, on her arrival at the fortress, 'fell down on her knees before the said lords, beseeching God to help her as she was not guilty of her accusement, and also desired the said lords to beseech the king's grace to be good unto her, and so they left her prisoner'. Anne was accused of adultery with a number of men of the court: Mark Smeaton, Henry Norris, Francis Weston and William Brereton. She was also accused of incest with her own brother, George Boleyn, Viscount Rochford. Anne who, as queen, was very rarely alone, would never have had the privacy to commit adultery on the occasions and with the number of men with whom it was alleged. She had strong religious beliefs and, before her death, swore her innocence on the sacrament, something that would have damned her soul if untrue. In spite of this she, along with the accused men, was tried and condemned to die, with Anne being sentenced to be burned or beheaded at the king's pleasure.

The queen had entirely lost her composure on arriving in the Tower and appeared hysterical, at times laughing and then breaking down into tears. Before her trial she also spoke unguardedly. It was her own words that had caused Francis Weston's arrest when she told the lieutenant of the Tower that 'she spoke to him because he did love her kinswoman Mrs Shelton and that she said he loves not his wife and he made answer to her again that he loved one in her house better than them both; she asked him who is that? To which he answered that it is yourself; and then she defied him'. She also spoke of Mark Smeaton, whom she had once found standing by the window in her chamber. When she asked him why he was sad, he said 'it was no matter', to which Anne – conscious of her position – replied, 'You may not look to have me speak to you as I should do a noble man, because you be an inferior person.' Smeaton had merely answered 'No, no, madam, a look sufficed.' The queen's ill-advised comments were used against both her and the men at their trials. By 17 May Anne had composed herself and, on hearing of the executions of the men with whom she was accused, she merely commented of Smeaton's death 'did he not exonerate me, before he died, of the public infamy he laid on me? Alas! I fear his soul will suffer for it.' Later that day she heard that her marriage to the king had been annulled.

As a small concession to the woman he had once loved so dearly, Henry delayed Anne's execution so that a swordsman could arrive from Calais to minister a more merciful death than beheading by axe. On the morning of 19 May the former queen made her way to a scaffold that had been erected on Tower Green. She turned to the crowd and made a carefully planned speech. According to her contemporary, Edward Hall, she declared:

Good Christian people, I am come hither to die, for according to the law and by the law I am judged to die, and therefore I will speak nothing against it. I am come hither to accuse no man, nor to speak any thing of that whereof I am accused and condemned to die, but I pray God save the king and send him long to reign over you, for a gentler nor a more merciful prince was there never: and to me he was ever a good, a gentle, and sovereign lord. And if any person will meddle of my cause, I require them to judge the best. And thus I take my leave of the world and of you all, and I heartily desire you all to pray for me. O Lord have mercy on me, to God I commend my soul.

Anne knelt on the straw of the scaffold and said loudly 'to Christ I commend my soul', as the headsman stepped up behind her and severed her head with a sword.

Before her death, Anne was aware that Henry had already selected his third wife and that her rival was waiting to assume her place. Anne Boleyn showed that it was possible for an Englishwoman to aspire to the throne. Unfortunately, in doing so, she laid the foundations for her own ruin by showing how to win the king and induce him towards marriage, an example that Henry's third wife, Jane Seymour, followed in her own pursuit of the king.

Family Regia, or *The Family of Henry VIII*, George Vertue 1742. This engraving shows Henry VII, his wife Elizabeth of York, his son Henry VIII and Henry VIII's favourite wife Jane Seymour. (Yale Centre for British Art)

Jane Seymour

Jane Seymour (*c.* 1508–37), the third wife of Henry VIII, is often considered to be the wife that he loved best. While, during her lifetime, Jane found her position as unstable as any of Henry's later queens, she died giving the king what he most ardently desired. Posthumously, in Henry's eyes, she became his favourite wife.

Jane was not born to be a queen and came from fairly humble origins. She was born around 1508 and was the eldest daughter of Sir John Seymour of Wolf Hall in Wiltshire and his wife, Margery Wentworth. Jane's father came from a family of local gentry but her mother was more distinguished, being a descendant of Edward III. More immediately, Margery's mother, Anne Say, had been the half-sister of Elizabeth Tylney, Countess of Surrey. Elizabeth Tylney was the mother of the 3rd Duke of Norfolk; Elizabeth Howard, the mother of Anne Boleyn; and Edmund Howard, the father of Catherine Howard. Nothing is recorded of Jane's childhood although she is likely to have been able to read and write. There is also evidence that she knew some French and that she was accomplished at needlework. At some point she joined the household of Catherine of Aragon.

It was from her service to Catherine that Jane gained her lifelong devotion to Princess Mary. Catherine retained a royal household until after her divorce in May 1533 and it is likely that Jane remained with her until then, missing out on an appointment with Anne Boleyn who had assembled her own royal household before April 1533. Around the middle of 1534, Jane's kinsman, Sir Francis Bryan, suggested a marriage for her with William Dormer, the only child of Sir Robert Dormer of Eythrope in Buckinghamshire. The Dormers were prominent and wealthy and it would have been a good match for Jane. According to the *Life of Jane Dormer*, a work commissioned by William's daughter, the Dormer family were less than happy with the lowly Jane. While Sir Robert was prepared to negotiate with the well-connected Bryan, his wife was determined that the match would not take place, taking steps to arrange a better match herself. William Dormer's hurried marriage with the higher-ranking Mary Sidney took place on 11 January 1535, ending Jane's hopes. Bryan, who felt some sense of responsibility for his Seymour kin, arranged another future for the young woman, securing a place for her with Anne Boleyn.

Jane Seymour by Hans Holbein.
(Stephen Porter)

Jane did not have wealth, status or looks to recommend her to a husband. The Imperial ambassador, Eustace Chapuys, described her as 'of middle stature and no great beauty, so fair that one would call her rather pale than otherwise'. While blond hair and pale skin was the contemporary ideal of beauty, Jane's surviving portraits do not compare favourably to those of other members of Henry's court. In spite of this, she was comely enough to attract the king as a potential mistress. It is probable that both Sir Francis Bryan and Jane's eldest brother, Edward Seymour, an experienced courtier, had this in mind for her.

During Anne Boleyn's time as queen, a number of women had been introduced to the king by the different factions at court in the hope that they would share his bed and gain political influence. In the summer of 1534 the so-called 'Imperial Lady' had enjoyed some success after becoming the king's mistress, obtaining better treatment for the king's eldest daughter, of whose party she was a member. Anne Boleyn's faction had retaliated with a pretty young girl of their own, Margaret Shelton. Sir Francis Bryan had previously been a partisan of Anne's but the pair had quarrelled. Jane was willing to put herself forward as Henry's mistress and, by January 1536, she and Anne Boleyn were rivals.

According to the antiquarian Thomas Fuller, Henry gave Jane a pendant containing his picture which she wore openly at court, causing Anne to snatch it from her enemy's neck with such violence that she hurt her hand. The *Life of Jane Dormer* suggests that Jane gave as good as she got and 'there was often much scratching and bye blows between the queen and her maid'. The crisis came in late

Jane Seymour's badge of the phoenix, together with the Tudor Rose, from a stained-glass window at the Seymour family home of Wolf Hall, near Marlborough. The glass is now in the nearby church of Great Bedwyn. (Elizabeth Norton)

January when Anne came upon Henry with Jane sitting on his knee, a sight that she blamed for her final miscarriage. This worked to Jane's advantage and, while she had apparently been happy to become the king's mistress, the relationship was in its early stages and she was still a virgin. With Anne's miscarriage, Jane and her supporters changed their objective and, as her rival had done before her, Jane made it clear that her price was marriage or nothing.

The first indication that Henry had of Jane's change of policy was when he sent her a purse of gold with a letter, which perhaps contained an invitation to join him in his bed. Jane

after kissing the letter, returned it unopened to the messenger, and throwing herself on her knees before him, begged the said messenger that he would pray the king on her part to consider that she was a gentlewoman of good and honourable parents, without reproach, and that she had no greater riches in the world than her honour, which she would not injure for a thousand deaths, and that if he wished to make her some present in money she begged it might be when God enabled her to make some honourable match.

Henry was smitten and vowed not to see her unchaperoned. Shortly afterwards, Edward Seymour and his wife were moved into apartments adjoining Henry's own so that he could regularly visit his new love. Jane was coached in how to behave by her supporters but she also greatly desired to be a queen herself and presented an appearance of quiet virtue to the king, the opposite of the fiery Anne Boleyn. By the end of April 1536 Henry and Jane had decided to marry and she was sent away from London to ensure that she was not implicated in the queen's fall. The day after Anne's death, the couple were betrothed, marrying on 30 May 1536.

Jane had come to prominence as part of an alliance between her family and the supporters of Princess Mary. She was fond of her unfortunate stepdaughter, who had been declared illegitimate with the divorce of her parents and banished from court. Even before her marriage, Jane had attempted to persuade Henry to recall Mary and, according to Eustace Chapuys, she

> proposed to him to replace the Princess to her former position; and on the king telling her that she must be out of her senses to think of such a thing, and that she ought to study the welfare and exaltation of her own children, if she had any by him, instead of looking for the good of others, the said Jane Seymour replied that in soliciting the Princess's reinstatement she thought she was asking for the good, the repose, and tranquillity of himself, of the children they themselves might have, and of the kingdom in general.

Jane raised the matter again once she had become queen, claiming that she needed someone of her own status to keep her company at court. Henry was more receptive, but he was determined to humble his daughter first and insisted that the price of her reinstatement was an acknowledgement of the invalidity of her parents' marriage and her own illegitimacy. Mary at first refused but on hearing that Henry intended to try her for treason she finally relented, agreeing to all he asked. For Jane, who was genuinely fond of Mary, this was excellent news and the girl was soon writing to her stepmother as 'the Queen's grace my good mother'.

Jane and Mary had much in common. In spite of the rise of the religious reform and the changes to the church, both remained staunchly attached to traditional religion. Martin Luther referred to Jane as 'an Enemy of the Gospel' and she was known to be no friend to Protestant reform. Her time as queen coincided with the beginnings of the Dissolution of the Monasteries, to which she was evidently opposed. Certainly, she attempted to save at least one nunnery from closure.

Henry was determined that Jane should not acquire political influence as his two previous wives had done, and he did not look kindly on any intervention

The royal arms of Henry VIII outside the Chapel Royal at Hampton Court, showing the entwined initials of Henry and Jane Seymour. Henry married Jane 'with indecent haste' after Anne Boleyn's execution. (Elizabeth Norton)

by her. In October 1536 a great rebellion against the religious changes broke out in Lincolnshire and soon spread to Yorkshire, where it was known as the Pilgrimage of Grace. This was the greatest threat to Henry's throne of his reign. He was therefore furious when Jane threw herself onto her knees before him and begged him to restore the dissolved religious houses, suggesting that 'perhaps God permitted this rebellion for ruining so many churches'. To the new queen's terror, her husband roared that 'he had often told her not to meddle with his affairs', before pointedly referring to the fate of Anne Boleyn.

For Jane, the idea that she might go the same way as her predecessor was terrifying and she made no further public political interventions during her time as queen. She did, however, attempt to ensure that no rival to her position emerged from within her own household. Jane was always depicted wearing the unflattering English gable hood, which entirely covered her hair and was shaped like the roof of a house. Although modest, the headdress was widely considered to be less comely than the more daring French hood, which had been favoured by Anne Boleyn. When Jane swore in a new, French educated, maid to her household, she insisted that the girl exchange her French hoods for gable hoods, even though the girl's friends complained they became her less well. For Jane, who had herself

Henry VIII in the statue above the main doors in the great gate of Trinity College, Cambridge. The college was founded by Henry in 1546. (Elizabeth Norton)

first attracted the king from within the queen's household, this was probably the point and she was widely considered to be a woman who was 'not very secure'.

When the queen attempted to intercede for the rebels in late 1536 she had been married to Henry for six months and still showed no signs of being pregnant. This was worrying for her, with rumours that her coronation was delayed until she had proved that she could bear a son. Finally, early in 1537, she realised that she was pregnant, to both her and Henry's joy. With her pregnancy, the king could not do enough for his third wife, obtaining the quails that she craved to eat from France and vowing to remain close to her side so that she was not frightened by any rumours.

Jane went into confinement at Hampton Court in September 1537 to await the birth of her child and finally, after a labour that lasted three days, she bore a healthy son on 12 October. The whole country erupted in rejoicing with news of the birth. For Henry, who had waited nearly thirty years for a male heir, Jane had fulfilled everything that was required of her. She was well enough to play a role in the christening of her son, who was named Edward, on 15 October but, soon afterwards, she fell ill with a fever. Thomas Cromwell later blamed those about her for her illness, claiming that 'our Mistress through the fault of them that were about her which suffered her to take great cold and to eat things that her fantasy in sickness called for'. It was most likely puerperal, or childbed, fever that killed

Edward VI as a child, Hans Holbein. (National Gallery of Art)

Edward VI as Prince of Wales. (Elizabeth Norton)

her. She became increasingly weak and, by 24 October, was barely conscious. She died that night, only twelve days after the birth of her son.

Jane Seymour's death was greeted with sorrow in England. Her stepdaughter, Mary, acted as chief mourner at the royal funeral that was held at Windsor. Henry VIII was also devastated, since Jane had died giving him his greatest desire. For a man who liked being married, his wife's death also created a void in his life, and within weeks, he had begun his search for a fourth bride.

Jane Seymour, Wenceslaus Hollar.
(Rijksmuseum)

Edward VI. (Elizabeth Norton)

4

Anne of Cleves

Anne of Cleves (1515–57) was not Henry VIII's first choice of bride. The death of Jane Seymour took him by surprise and, aware that England was dangerously isolated in Europe, he wanted a foreign wife. His first choice was a French alliance, but when this came to nothing he turned to the Imperial royal family, his choice settling on the teenaged Christina of Denmark, the niece of the Emperor Charles V and great-niece of Catherine of Aragon. Christina was unenthusiastic and, by the end of 1538, negotiations had ended unsuccessfully. Dangerously, France and the Empire had by then concluded an alliance. Henry decided to approach the Protestant Schmalkaldic League of Germany whose founder, John Frederick, Elector of Saxony, had an unmarried sister-in-law: Anne of Cleves.

Anne of Cleves was the second of four children born to John, Duke of Cleves, and his wife, Maria of Juliers. She was born at Dusseldorf on 22 September 1515. Anne's lineage was noble since she was descended from Edward III of England, as well as being closely related to Louis XII of France and to the Imperial royal family. Her father ruled the German dukedoms of Cleves and Mark, while her mother was the heiress of the larger duchies of Juliers and Berg. The marriage of Anne's parents created a strategically important territory on both sides of the Rhine and this prestige was further increased by the acquisition of the dukedom of Ghelders by Anne's brother, William, an inheritance that was disputed by the Emperor Charles V and brought the two into conflict. Contrary to common belief, Anne's family were not Protestants and, while her father had some interest in reform and did not recognise the authority of the pope, her mother raised her daughters in accordance with the traditional faith. Anne's eldest sister, Sibylla, was married to John Frederick, Elector of Saxony, one of the founders of the Schmalkaldic League, a Protestant defensive league in opposition to the Holy Roman Empire. As a Catholic state, Cleves was not a member, but its links were close enough to ensure that Anne was the best match the League could offer.

Anne of Cleves's upbringing was strict. According to the report of Nicholas Wotton, the English ambassador there, she

> hath from her childhood (like as the lady Sybille was, till she were married, and the lady Amelia hath been and is) been brought up with the lady Duchess her mother, and in manner never from her elbow, the lady Duchess being a wise

Christina of Denmark, Duchess of Milan, by Hans Holbein. Christina's portrait enchanted Henry and she became his first choice as his fourth wife. (Elizabeth Norton)

lady, and one that very straightly looketh to her children. All the gentlemen of the court, and other that I have asked of, rapport her [Anne] to be of very lowly and gentle conditions, by the which she hath so much won her mother's favour, that she is very loath to suffer her to depart from her.

Anne's upbringing, overseen by her strict mother, was far from that which English noblewomen could expect to receive in the same period. Although the education of women had become fashionable in much of Europe, the movement had failed to penetrate as far as Cleves. Anne received a very limited education. She could read and write but knew no language other than German. She was skilled in needlework but knew nothing of music. In spite of this, the English ambassador in 1539 noted encouragingly that 'her wit is so good, that no doubt she will in a short space learn the English tongue, when so ever she putteth her mind to it'. Politically, Anne was a highly suitable bride, with the match first suggested at the end of 1537, only weeks after Jane Seymour's death. Negotiations began in earnest in early 1539, while the marriage treaty had been agreed by the end of September. After a long journey in foul weather, Anne arrived in England at the end of December accompanied by a large retinue. By New Year's Day she had reached Rochester where Henry, impatient to see his new bride, decided to visit her.

The portrait of Anne of Cleves that Hans Holbein painted for Henry. Although Henry had asked for the portrait to be as accurate as possible, he was disappointed when he met Anne, believing that she was not as attractive as the painting. (Jonathan Reeve, JR822b53fp414 15001550)

Above and below: Anne of Cleves. Anne's elaborate German clothes drew critical comments when she arrived in England. (Jonathan Reeve, JR1113 15001550, Elizabeth Norton)

Henry VIII enjoyed being married and, by the time of Anne's arrival in England, he imagined that he was already in love with her. At the end of 1537 his ambassador to Brussels had commented of Anne that 'there is no great praise either of her personage or beauty' but, otherwise, Henry had received nothing but good reports of her appearance. A portrait produced by Hans Holbein on Henry's instructions during the marriage negotiations looks comely enough. A description of Anne at the time of her marriage by Marillac, the French ambassador, suggests that she was no great beauty, appearing rather older than expected. She was, however, 'tall and very assured in carriage and countenance, showing that in her turn and vivacity of wit supplies the place of beauty'. Henry's chief minister, Thomas Cromwell, also thought that she had a queenly manner. Anne was later considered to be prettier than Catherine Parr, Henry's sixth wife. In spite of her reputation, she was very far from ugly, but she was no beauty. The main problem may have been her clothes, which were heavy and highly unfashionable in England, with Marillac commenting of Anne and her ladies that they were so badly dressed 'they would be thought ugly even if they were beautiful'. Be that as it may, by 1540 Henry VIII was approaching fifty, bald and was grossly overweight with an ulcerous leg. Of the pair, it was Anne who received the worst surprise in her spouse.

In accordance with romantic tradition, the king visited his bride in disguise, dressed as a messenger. He entered the chamber to find his fiancée standing at a window, staring down at a bull baiting in the courtyard below. Anne had received many visitors since her arrival in England, and paid the stranger little heed, studiously looking out the window even as he embraced her. After failing to get any attention from his new queen, the king was forced to leave the room to change, putting on a kingly purple coat. When he re-entered the room, this was the sign for everyone to suddenly 'recognise' him and, as the people around her fell to their knees, Anne realised her mistake, bowing before her future husband. Henry appeared to take it all in good part, taking her by the hand and leading her to another chamber, where they 'talked together lovingly' that evening. However, he left for London as soon as the tide changed the next day, forgetting to give Anne her New Year's gift of fine furs and sables. While he probably never actually complained that he had been brought a 'Flanders Mare', rather than a woman, he was dismayed with his bride. On the boat, he complained loudly that 'I see nothing in this woman as men report of her; and I marvel that wise men would make such report as they have done'. Anne was oblivious to his reaction to her and she continued her journey to London, being received publicly by the king at Blackheath on 3 January.

Henry, terrified of offending Anne's brother or brother-in-law, continued to show his commitment to the marriage in public. In private, however, he instructed his councillors to find some way out of the match, leaving them frantically busy in the days before the wedding. The council focussed on a childhood betrothal between Anne and the son of the Duke of Lorraine but, when the ambassadors from Cleves swore that it had been broken off and the future queen herself gave an oath that she was free to marry, there was nothing more that could be done. Henry went to the wedding on 5 January with bad grace, complaining to Cromwell that 'I must needs against my will put my neck in the yoke'. Attempts to consummate the marriage were disastrous with Henry finding himself impotent on the wedding night and every subsequent night that they spent together.

For Henry, the marriage was an absolute disaster, but Anne's thoughts are less clear. In June 1540, three of Anne's ladies, ladies Rutland, Rochford and Edgecombe, reported a conversation that they had apparently had with her around Midsummer. According to their report, Anne insisted that she was not yet pregnant, although denied that she was a virgin, asking, 'How can I be a maid, and sleep every night with the king?' Lady Rochford pointed out, 'There must be more than that,' to which the queen replied, 'When he comes to bed he kisses me, and taketh me by the hand, and biddeth me, Good night, sweetheart: and in the morning kisses me, and biddeth me, Farewell, darling. Is not this enough?' Lady Rutland gently chided, 'Madam there must be more than this, or it will be long before we have a Duke of York, which all this realm most desireth.' But Anne merely asked again, 'Is not this enough? I am contented with this, for I know no more.'

This is usually taken as evidence that Anne was unaware of the troubles in her marriage but it must be considered suspect. As late as July 1540 Anne's chancellor, Lord Rutland, required an interpreter to speak to Anne and it is unlikely that she had a sufficient command of English for such an intimate conversation. More likely, the conversation was fabricated at the time of Anne's divorce in order to support the king's position. The couple's marital difficulties were well known and Cromwell, whose own fall was caused by his promotion of the marriage, begged Anne's servants to make her appear more pleasing to the king. The queen also desperately tried to speak to the minister, suggesting she was aware that something was very wrong.

By the end of June 1540, Henry had decided to end his marriage to Anne. He was, by that time, deeply involved in an affair with one of her ladies, Catherine Howard. The political situation in Europe also made an alliance with Cleves much less favourable than it had been. As a first step towards divorce, Anne was sent to Richmond, ostensibly to keep her safe from the plague. Once separated, Henry ordered a church court to rule on the marriage's validity based on Anne's earlier betrothal to Francis of Lorraine, non-consummation and his own lack of consent to the match. In the early hours of 6 July a messenger arrived at Richmond to speak to Anne, waking her. She sent for her brother's ambassador, Carl Harst, and, around 4 a.m., summoned her chancellor, Rutland. The king's message, which asked her to consent to her marriage being examined, struck the queen speechless and she meekly agreed to the trial. While she is usually considered to have taken her divorce well, in reality, she was terrified, remembering the fates of Catherine of Aragon and Anne Boleyn.

The result of the hearing was a foregone conclusion and, on 7 July, the assembled clergymen ruled that 'the king and Anne of Cleves were nowise bound

Thomas Cromwell, Jacob Houbraken after Hans Holbein. (Rijksmuseum)

by the marriage solemnised between them'. Henry then sent commissioners to his former wife, in order to obtain her agreement to the annulment. The commissioners claimed that Anne received the news calmly but, according to the seventeenth-century historian Edward Herbert, on their arrival she fainted, perhaps fearing imminent arrest. Harst had also spoken to her shortly before the commissioners arrived, listening to her insisting that she would remain Henry's wife until death parted them. According to Harst, Anne cried and screamed so much that it broke his heart to hear her. This was never communicated to Henry, but it accounts for Anne's later attempts to be reinstated as queen after Catherine Howard's death and to annul her divorce during the reign of Mary I.

While Anne never privately accepted the divorce, she had no desire to be a second Anne Boleyn and agreed to write to the king, setting out her consent to all that happened:

> It may please your majesty to know that, though this case must needs be most hard and sorrowful unto me, for the great love which I bear to your most noble person, yet, having more regard to God and his trust than to any world affection, as it beseemed me, at the beginning, to submit me to such examination and determination of the said clergy, whom I have and do accept for judges competent in that behalf. So now being ascertained how the same clergy hath therein given judgement and sentence, I knowledge myself hereby to accept and approve the same, wholly and entirely putting myself, for my state and condition, to your highness' goodness and pleasure; most humbly beseeching your Majesty that, though it be determined that the pretended matrimony between us is void and of none effect, whereby I neither can nor will repute myself your Grace's wife, considering this sentence (whereunto I stand) and your Majesty's clean and pure living with me, yet it will please you to take me for one of your most humble servants, and so to determine of me, as I may sometimes have the fruition of your most noble presence; which as I shall esteem for a great benefit, so, my lords and others of your Majesty's council, now being with me, have put me in comfort thereof; and that your highness will take me for your sister; for the which I most humbly thank you accordingly.

She tactfully signed her letter as 'Anne, the daughter of Cleves'. Anne acquitted herself cleverly in the divorce and Henry was so relieved that he assigned her a huge divorce settlement, granting her the palaces of Richmond and Bletchingley, as well as a number of other properties and a generous annual allowance. For the remainder of Henry's life, Anne lived in comfort as a rich and independent single woman, even visiting court and dining with her former husband in private. The couple found they got on so well that groundless rumours abounded that they had rekindled their relationship and that Anne had even borne the king children.

Following Henry's death there was less necessity to ensure that she continued to accept the terms of her divorce and Edward VI's council stripped her of many of her properties, including her two principal residences. She also found that, with high inflation, her pension was of little value and she lived in poverty, desperate to return to Cleves. Anne's position improved somewhat in 1553 with the accession of her friend, Mary I. She made her last public appearance at Mary's coronation, riding in the same chariot as Princess Elizabeth. This renewed royal favour did not last long, however. Perhaps due to her friendship with the princess, Anne found herself under suspicion during the rebellion of Sir Thomas Wyatt the Younger early in 1554, which also led to Elizabeth's imprisonment in the Tower. No evidence could be found against her but the former queen appeared less frequently at court. She continued to live independently and was the last survivor of Henry VIII's six wives, dying in Chelsea on 15 July 1557.

Anne of Cleves is often called the luckiest of Henry VIII's wives. She used her intelligence to survive a very difficult situation but her brief marriage blighted her life and her craving to return to her homeland was never fulfilled. She was, however, certainly luckier than her successor as queen, the unfortunate Catherine Howard.

King Henry VIII from King's College, Cambridge. Founded by Henry VI in 1441, it was finally finished in 1544 during the reign of Henry VIII. (Elizabeth Norton)

5

Catherine Howard

Catherine Howard (*c.* 1521/25–42) was a cousin of Anne Boleyn's and followed her unfortunate predecessor to the block. Her date of birth is nowhere recorded, but she was young when she became queen and it was probably between 1521 and 1525. She was the daughter of Lord Edmund Howard, a younger brother of the Duke of Norfolk, and his wife, Joyce Culpeper. Catherine's mother died while she was still a young child and her father died in 1539, having spent the previous two years absent from England as mayor of Calais. Catherine, who was the youngest in a large family, had little contact with either of her parents. She was raised in the household of her father's stepmother, Agnes Tylney, Dowager Duchess of Norfolk, at her homes in Horsham and Lambeth.

The duchess's household was home to a number of young girls and Catherine mixed with both gentlewomen, such as herself, and servants, sharing a dormitory room with the other unmarried women. She was taught to read and write, but received little further education. The duchess was aware that Catherine, whose father was virtually penniless, needed to attract a rich husband. Hoping that her pretty young granddaughter would prove to be musical, she arranged for a neighbour, Henry Manox, to teach her to play the virginals. In spite of her pennilessness, Catherine was a member of one of the premier noble families in England and Manox was far beneath her socially. He seduced the young girl and, according to his later testimony, they fell in love with each other. Such an association was all too common in the duchess's household but, when it was brought to her attention, she was furious, beating Catherine and ordering the couple to separate when she caught them together one day. In spite of the duchess's prohibition, the relationship continued and, while they stopped short of sexual intercourse, they enjoyed an intimate relationship. Catherine herself later admitted that 'at the flattering and fair persuasions of Manox being but a young girl suffered him at sundry times to handle and touch the secret parts of my body which neither became me with honesty to permit nor him to require'. Manox was dismissed when the duchess caught him and Catherine alone in her chapel chamber. Probably hoping to marry his high-ranking young love, he followed the household when it moved to Lambeth.

Catherine lost interest in Manox at Lambeth when she met a young kinsman of hers, Francis Dereham. Although not of equal status to a Howard daughter,

Catherine Howard. Catherine was the youngest and prettiest of Henry's wives and Anne was unable to compete with her. (Elizabeth Norton)

Dereham was higher born than the lowly Manox. He was also young and handsome and a particular favourite of Catherine's step-grandmother, who flirted with him herself. Many of the girls in the duchess's household had lovers and, while the maidens' dormitory was locked at night, the key was easily stolen. The young men of the household were then free to come and go, entertaining their lovers with picnics before joining them in bed. Catherine had been very young at the time of her flirtation with Manox, but when she met Dereham she was a teenager ready for a full affair. She later admitted that

> Frances Dereham by many persuasions procured me to his vicious purpose and obtained first to lie upon my bed with his doublet and hose and after within the bed and finally he lay with me naked and used me in such sort as a man doth his wife many and sundry times but how often I know not and our company ended almost a year before the King's majesty was married to my lady Anne of Cleves and continued not past one quarter of a year or little above.

To Catherine, growing up in the lax atmosphere of her grandmother's household, such conduct seemed natural. She lost her virginity to Dereham, who later claimed that the pair became engaged. Catherine, proud of her higher status, admitted to a sexual relationship with her young suitor, but denied any promise of marriage. She still expected to be well married, although the couple referred to each other as husband and wife and exchanged love tokens. Dereham also lent Catherine the substantial sum of £100, something which again suggests that he hoped his seduction would lead to marriage.

There was little privacy in the duchess's household, with the affair soon common knowledge. Henry Manox, who was still hovering at the edge of the household, was jealous, writing to Catherine's step-grandmother to set out the details of the affair. Rather than passing it directly to the duchess, he left it on her pew in her private chapel where Catherine found it and showed it to Dereham. The precaution of destroying the letter was perhaps not necessary as the dowager already knew of the relationship. According to Katherine Tylney, one of the girls in the household, the duchess once 'found Dereham embracing Mrs Katherine Howard in his arms and kissing her, and thereat was much offended and gave Dereham a blow, and also beat the Queen [Catherine] and gave Joan Bulmer a blow because she was present. When Dereham was wanted the Duchess would say, "I warrant you if you seek him in Katherine Howard's chamber you shall find him there."' The duchess apparently felt that, providing her granddaughter's conduct did not disturb her peace, it was not her responsibility. She did, however, ask her son to speak to Catherine about what was expected of a Howard.

Catherine forgot all about her affair with Dereham when her uncle, the Duke of Norfolk, secured a place for her in the household of Anne of Cleves. She arrived at court towards the end of 1539 to assist with the preparations for the new queen. It is possible that Norfolk selected Catherine over her cousins and sisters for her pretty appearance. Marillac, the French ambassador, described her as 'a lady of great beauty', although he later qualified this by saying that she was more graceful than beautiful and very short – she was so young she may not even have finished growing. Norfolk probably intended his niece to attract a high-profile husband rather than the king as, in December 1539, Henry was still very much looking forward to the arrival of Anne of Cleves. With his disappointment in his bride, the king began looking around the women of his court and his eye was caught by Catherine. Once this interest became obvious to the Howards, they coached her to present an air of youthful purity. Henry's infatuation was soon public knowledge at court. According to one report:

This was first whispered by the courtiers, who observed the king to be much taken with another young lady of very diminutive stature, whom he now has. It is a certain fact, that about the same time many citizens of London saw the king very frequently in the day-time, and sometimes at midnight, pass over to her on the river Thames in a little boat. The Bishop of Winchester also very often provided feastings and entertainments for them in his palace; but the citizens regarded all this not as a sign of divorcing the queen, but of adultery.

Catherine was always in her element at court festivities, loving the attention that she received. In spite of the rumours about her relationship with Henry, it is unlikely that it was consummated. The king was convinced that his pretty young bride was a virgin when they married on 28 July 1540, shortly after his divorce.

Thomas Howard, 3rd Duke of Norfolk, uncle of Anne Boleyn and Catherine Howard, Lucas Vorsterman after Hans Holbein. (Rijksmuseum)

Catherine was determined to enjoy herself as queen and Henry showered her with presents. Over Christmas and New Year 1540–1, she received many fine gifts of jewellery, including a square-shaped jewel containing twenty-seven table diamonds and twenty-six clusters of pearls and a muffler of black velvet covered in gems. That New Year, Henry and Catherine received a visit at Hampton Court from Anne of Cleves and, after some uncertainty over how the new queen should receive her predecessor, the pair got on well. Catherine and Anne danced together and, when Henry sent his new wife a present of a ring and two small dogs, she presented them to Anne. Catherine had her own barge, which she made use of in her ceremonial entry to London in early 1541.

Henry's marriage to Catherine rejuvenated him and he called her his 'jewel'. He could not stop time indefinitely and, in March 1541, his leg ulcer, which had troubled him since his marriage to Anne Boleyn, suddenly closed, putting him in danger of his life. Fearing impending death, the suddenly aged king barred the queen from his presence, the first sign of trouble in their marriage. In May 1541 Catherine complained to Henry that she had heard a rumour that she was to be set aside in favour of Anne of Cleves. He reassured her by saying that 'even if he had to marry again, he would never retake Mme de Cleves'. His failure to rule out any future marriage cannot have put her mind at rest.

Detail from the window of King Solomon and the Queen of Sheba in King's College Chapel, Cambridge. Some say that the image of the Queen of Sheba is modelled on Catherine Howard. This stained glass was created during Henry VIII's reign and paid for by Henry himself. (Elizabeth Norton)

Henry VIII in the prime of life. After the celebrated cartoon by Hans Holbein. (Jonathan Reeve, JR955b53piv 15001600)

Henry was over thirty years older than Catherine and a poor physical specimen. Although she was in awe of her husband, she was not in love with him. She was, in fact, already in love with someone else at the time of her marriage. Catherine met Thomas Culpeper shortly after she arrived at court. He was a member of Henry's privy chamber and a man who would have been considered an entirely suitable husband for her. He was young and handsome and the couple may already have been lovers before Catherine became queen. They certainly became lovers after her marriage. The queen's only surviving letter, written around April 1541, is a testament to her love for Culpeper:

Master Culpeper, I heartily recommend me unto you, praying you to send me word how that you do. It was showed me that you was sick, the which thing troubled me very much till such time that I hear from you praying you to send me word how that you do, for I never longed so much for [a] thing as I do to see you and to speak with you, the which I trust shall be shortly now. The which doth comfortly me very much when I think of it, and when I think again that you shall depart from me again it makes my heart to die to think what fortune I have that I cannot be always in your company. It my trust is always in you that you will be as you have promised me, and in that hope I trust upon it still, praying that you will come when my Lady Rochford is here for then I shall be best at leisure to be at your commandment, thanking you for that you have promised me to be so good unto that poor fellow my man which is one of the griefs that I do feel to depart from him for then I do know no one that I dare trust to send to you, and therefore I pray you take him to be with you that I may sometimes hear from you one thing. I pray you to give me a horse for my man for I had much ado to get one and therefore I pray send me one by him and in so doing I am as I said afor, and thus I take my leave of you, trusting to see you shortly again and I would you was with me now that you might see what pain I take in writing to you.

She signed her letter, 'Yours as long as life endures.' Committing details of her affair to writing was not wise, but the lovers were incapable of allaying suspicions. Soon after her marriage, Catherine's maids noticed her giving loving glances to Culpeper out of the window. She also barred them from her chamber at certain times, admitting only her kinswoman Lady Rochford, who was the widow of George Boleyn.

Catherine relied on Lady Rochford to help her and Culpeper meet in secret throughout her marriage. In her own examination, Catherine confessed that 'my lady Rochford would at every lodging search the back doors & tell her of them if there were any'. Henry and Catherine left London on 30 June 1541 for a progress to the north of England. Culpeper, as one of Henry's gentlemen, was present, with the couple seeing no reason to curtail their relationship during the trip. According, again, to Catherine's examination, in which she denied any impropriety, one night Culpeper met her in a chamber off the stairs at Lincoln and on other occasions the pair met in her bedchamber. During the assignations, Lady Rochford would sit apart with her back to them. She sometimes fell asleep.

Catherine remained oblivious to any danger when the court returned to Windsor on 26 October 1541, continuing her affair by meeting her lover in a kitchen at the castle. The queen, who was believed to represent the traditional religion's party at court, had many enemies. Soon after the court's return, Archbishop Cranmer was approached by John Lassells, an ardent religious reformer who had shocking information. Lassells' sister, Mary Hall, had been a member of the Dowager Duchess of Norfolk's household at the same time as Catherine. When her brother suggested that she approach the queen for a post, she had refused, telling him that the queen was 'light of living'. Mary Hall was able to give him the details of Catherine's relationships with Manox and Dereham. Cranmer was shocked by this and put everything in a letter, passing it to the king on 2 November. Henry was devastated, refusing to believe it. He was also furious and, in order to clear Catherine's name, ordered that an investigation be carried out. His wife knew nothing of the investigation but, under pressure, Manox confessed. On 4 November 1541, guards burst into the queen's room as she was practising her dancing steps, telling her that 'it is no more time to dance'. Under interrogation, she confessed to her relationships with Manox and Dereham. Both the affairs ended before Catherine's marriage and the Dowager Duchess of Norfolk, for one, predicted that the worst that would happen would be that the marriage was annulled and her granddaughter sent home in disgrace. Within days however, Culpeper's name had been mentioned and, on 11 November, Catherine was sent as a prisoner to Syon House.

The evidence of Catherine's relationship with Culpeper was much more dangerous than her earlier affairs, since adultery in a queen was high treason. Catherine always denied that her relationship with Culpeper was a sexual one, while she, her lover and Lady Rochford all sought to blame each other in an attempt to save themselves. They were unsuccessful and Dereham and Culpeper were executed on 10 December 1541. Catherine still hoped that she would escape with her life but, on 16 January 1542, Parliament opened in London and condemned the queen and Lady Rochford to death without trial.

On 10 February, Catherine was taken by water to the Tower of London. During the evening of 12 February, she was told that she would be executed the next day. She had spent her time in the Tower weeping but, on hearing that she was soon to die, the queen composed herself, asking for the block to be brought to her so that she could practice for the morning. The next day, both Catherine Howard and Lady Rochford were led to a scaffold on Tower Green. Catherine was so weak that she could hardly speak. After being helped onto the scaffold, she made no speech, confessing only that she deserved to die. Still trembling with terror, she knelt and placed her head on the block before being beheaded with an axe. Her body was hurriedly cleared away to make space on the block for Lady Rochford.

Catherine Howard almost certainly died before her twentieth birthday. Unlike Anne Boleyn, she was probably guilty of the crimes of which she was accused. She was entirely unsuited for the role of queen and Henry VIII must bear much of the blame for her terrible end. In his sixth wife, Catherine Parr, he chose more wisely.

The Tower of London. The Norman White Tower at the Tower of London was the place where many political and religious dissidents were housed before execution. (Courtesy of Stephen Porter)

The Traitors' Gate at the Tower of London, through which Anne Boleyn, Catherine Howard and Elizabeth I passed on their way to prison. (Elizabeth Norton)

The Chapel of St Peter ad Vincula in the Tower of London. The remains of many victims of Tudor treason trials were buried here, among them Anne Boleyn, Catherine Howard, Jane Grey, Thomas Cromwell, Thomas More and John Fisher. (Elizabeth Norton)

Catherine Parr. Engraving after Hans Holbein. (Courtesy of the Lewis Walpole Library, Yale University)

6

Catherine Parr

Catherine Parr (1512–48), the sixth wife of Henry VIII, is remembered as the wife who survived, but she came close to disaster during her marriage. Only her intelligence and quick thinking saved the situation, ensuring that she was the last wife of England's most married monarch. Like her predecessor, she was not born royal and was, instead, the eldest surviving child of Sir Thomas Parr of Kendal and his wife, Matilda, or Maude, Green. She was born in 1512 and was named after Catherine of Aragon, who was probably her godmother.

Catherine's parents enjoyed solid court careers and were in high favour with the king. The family was rocked by the sudden death of Thomas Parr on 11 November 1517, leaving his widow to raise three young children alone. Maude Parr was a remarkable woman and defied expectations that she would remarry, instead maintaining her position as a lady in waiting to the queen. She was ambitious for her children and provided them with a good education, with a letter from Lord Dacre to his son-in-law Lord Scrope recommending that his son be raised in Maude's household 'for I assure you he might learn with her as in any place that I know, as well nature, as French and other languages, which me seems were a commodious thing'.

Maude would very much have liked to be placed in charge of the education of young Henry Scrope. She sought ambitious marriages for her children and, in 1523, opened negotiations for Catherine to marry the boy, who was his father's heir. Maude, who was on friendly terms with his grandfather, Lord Dacre, agreed the match with him before approaching Lord Scrope. This proved to be a mistake since Scrope resented his father-in-law's interference and was unenthusiastic. Undaunted, Catherine's mother wrote to Lord Dacre to complain:

> Where it pleased you at your last being here to take pain in the matter in consideration of marriage between the Lord Scrope's son and my daughter Catherine, for the which I heartily thank you; at which time I thought the matter in good furtherance. How be it, I perceive that my said Lord Scrope is not agreeable to that consideration, as more plainly may appear unto you by certain articles sent to me from my said lord; the copy of which articles I send you herein enclosed. My lord's pleasure is to have a full answer from me before Lammas next coming, wherefore it may please you to be so good to have this

Catherine Parr's badge, from a stained-glass window in the chapel at Sudeley Castle. Sudeley was Lord Thomas Seymour's principal residence. (Elizabeth Norton)

matter in your remembrance, for I perceive well this matter is not like to take effect except it be by your help.

Lord Dacre admired Maude and was enthusiastic about the match, convincing her to persevere. He also attempted to persuade his son-in-law, pointing out that

I cannot see, without that ye would marry him to one heir of land, which will be right costly, that ye can marry him to so good a stock as my lady Parr, for divers considerations, first, is remembering the wisdom of my said lady, and the good wise stock of the Greens whereof she is come, and also of the wise stock of the Parrs of Kendal, for all which men do look when they do marry their child, to the wisdom of the blood of that they do marry with.

Lord Scrope still refused to countenance the match and, eventually, Maude admitted defeat. She continued to seek advantageous marriages for her children and, in 1527, secured Anne Bourchier, heiress to the Earl of Essex, for her son William. Maude impoverished herself in purchasing this match and was forced to lower her hopes for her eldest daughter. By 1529 at the latest, Catherine had married Edward Burgh, the young son and heir of Sir Thomas Burgh of Gainsborough Hall in Lincolnshire. The marriage was brief and there is little surviving evidence of Catherine's time in Lincolnshire. She was widowed in early 1533.

Catherine's second marriage was more lasting than her first. By the end of 1533 she had married John Neville, Lord Latimer, a widower in his forties. It was a good match for the young widow and she became mistress of Snape Castle in Yorkshire, taking on the upbringing of her two stepchildren. Although she soon established a motherly relationship with her stepdaughter, Margaret Neville, Catherine's time in Yorkshire was not wholly happy. She became personally caught up in the events of the Pilgrimage of Grace, the great northern rebellion against Henry VIII's changes to the church. Catherine was an adherent of the reformed faith and is unlikely to have had any sympathies with the rebels. Latimer, however, was staunchly traditional in his beliefs. When a mob arrived at Snape Castle in October 1536 demanding that he become one of the rebellion's leaders, he went with them. His wife quickly began to hear reports of her husband's conduct and it must have been a very worrying time for her. Although Latimer joined the rebels under duress, once in command he proved energetic, dangerously asking the Archbishop of York and clergy 'to show their learning whether subjects might lawfully move war in any case against their prince'.

Latimer's conduct sounded like treason to Henry VIII and when the rebels dispersed, following the promise of a royal pardon, Catherine's husband set out southwards to explain himself. This pleased no-one, with the king ordering him to remain in the north until called for. More immediately worrying, the rebels saw Latimer's conduct as a betrayal. In early 1537 an armed group arrived at Snape, forcing their way into the castle and taking Catherine and her stepchildren hostage. Latimer, who was far from home, was frantic, writing that the rebels had threatened to destroy the house if he did not return home quickly and that 'if I do not please them I know not what they will do with my body and goods, wife and children'. He was in a difficult position, since he could not risk rejoining the rebels given the king's anger. He begged for leave to rescue his family, as well as asking Henry if 'I might live on such small lands as I have in the South', since he would then 'little care of my lands in the North'. Finally, Latimer rushed to Snape and persuaded the rebels to let his family go. He remained in disgrace with the king for some time but had returned to royal favour before his death in March 1543, by which time the couple were often resident in London.

Lord Latimer left Catherine comparatively wealthy. It is unlikely that she expected a lengthy widowhood as she already had two suitors by the time of her second husband's death. In a letter written by Catherine in 1547, she wrote, 'I would not have you think that this mine honest goodwill towards you to proceed of any sudden motion of passion; for, as truly as God is God, my mind was fully bent, the other time I was at liberty, to marry you before any man I know.' The object of her affection was Thomas Seymour, the brother of Jane Seymour and a very substantial man. Seymour had spent much time on the Continent on the king's service but returned to court in January 1543. The only evidence for Catherine and Seymour's relationship in 1543 comes from their later letters, but it was evidently passionate, with the couple deciding to marry once Catherine was free. Thomas was only a few years older than the young widow and very handsome. After two arranged marriages, Catherine looked forward to making her own choice.

Unfortunately for the couple, Catherine had another suitor in early 1543. Her mother had served Catherine of Aragon, something that had ensured that the young Catherine had been chosen to share Princess Mary's childhood lessons. By 16 February 1543, Catherine had renewed her acquaintance with the princess. On that date the king paid a tailor's bill addressed to Lord Latimer's widow for fabrics for Italian, French, Dutch and Venetian style gowns, as well as pleats and sleeves, hoods and other items of clothing. The clothes were for both Catherine and Mary and the fact that Henry settled the bill is the first indication of his interest in Lady Latimer. Henry also became unusually attentive to his daughter at around the same time, with Chapuys noting that 'the king has shown the greatest possible affection and liberality to the Princess, and not a day passes but he goes to visit her in her chamber two or three times with the utmost cordiality'. The object of Henry's interest was not Mary and, to her horror, Catherine soon discovered that it was her. When Henry's interest became clear, Seymour took a step back. Perhaps to ensure that the field was clear, the king appointed his rival as his ambassador in Brussels in May 1543.

By 1543, Henry VIII, with his disastrous marital history, was a terrifying figure. Catherine was reluctant when she first received his proposal of marriage, replying boldly that 'it were better to be your mistress than your wife'. Her suitor was, however, adamant that the pretty widow should become his sixth wife. As Catherine considered ways to avoid this fate, she had a religious experience, later writing, 'God withstood my will therein most vehemently for a time, and through his grace and goodness, made that possible which seemed to me most impossible; that was, made me renounce utterly mine own will, and to follow his will most willingly.' She believed that God called her to become queen so that she could promote the religious reform. The couple were married on 13 July 1543.

In spite of her apprehension about her marriage, Catherine and Henry did become close, with the king referring to his latest bride as 'Kate' or 'Sweetheart'. Catherine also grew fond of her third husband, writing, in the summer of 1544, when they were apart,

Catherine Parr. (Elizabeth Norton)

Although the discourse of time and account of days neither is long nor many of your Majesty's absence, yet the want of your presence, so much beloved and desired of me, maketh me, that I cannot quietly pleasure in any thing, until I hear from your Majesty. The time therefore seemeth to me very long with a great desire to know how your Highness has done, since your departing hence. Whose prosperity and health I prefer and desire more than mine own. And whereas I know your Majesty's absence is never without great respects of things most convenient and necessary, yet love and affection compelled me to desire your presence. And again, the same zeal and love forceth me also to be best content with that which is your will and pleasure, and to embrace most joyfully his will and pleasure whom I love. God, the knower of secrets, can judge these words not to be only written with ink, but most truly impressed in the heart.

Henry showed great trust in Catherine by appointing her to act as regent during his campaign in France in the summer of 1544. She relished the challenge that this offered, playing an active role in ensuring the security of the northern border of England. She also arranged supplies for Henry in France.

Catherine Parr is mainly remembered for her domestic role. While the tradition that she nursed Henry in his illnesses is likely to be exaggerated, she did show a great interest in her three royal stepchildren, Mary, Elizabeth and Edward. Catherine was often in the company of Princess Mary and they had a close relationship as friends. The pair regularly exchanged gifts and had a number of similar interests, including dancing and a love of fine clothes. The queen also took an active role in the education and upbringing of her younger stepchildren, with both Elizabeth and Edward quickly coming to refer to her as their mother. A letter of Elizabeth's to Catherine from July 1544 shows the princess's devotion, when she wrote that fortune 'has deprived me for a whole year of your most illustrious presence, and not thus content, has yet again robbed me of the same good, which thing would be intolerable to me, did I not hope to enjoy it very soon'. Elizabeth had been sent away from court following Catherine's wedding under something of a cloud, but the queen, through her endeavours with the king, was eventually able to secure her return to court.

Catherine was a great influence on Elizabeth, particularly concerning religion. She used her position as queen to promote the reformed faith, publishing her own religious work, *Prayers or Meditation*, during her marriage. She also prepared a more radical work, *A Lamentation of a Sinner*, although she was unable to publish this until after Henry's death. The queen patronised a translation of Erasmus's *Paraphrases of the Gospel*, a work for which she obtained the Catholic Princess Mary's translation services. This was particularly impressive given the fact that the work was condemned as heretical in Mary's reign and shows the princess's love for her stepmother. Catherine was able to perform a service to both her stepdaughters by including them in the family circle. Finally, in February 1544, the Third Act of Succession was passed, bringing both princesses back into the succession, although both still remained illegitimate.

While Catherine had been fearful about marrying Henry, over time she became bolder, seeking to convert him to the religious reform. Although the king had engineered the break with Rome, he remained largely traditional in his religious beliefs and was by no means a Protestant. Catherine's religious beliefs earned her enemies at court, the most dangerous of which were Stephen Gardiner, Bishop of Winchester, and Thomas Wriothesley, Henry's Lord Chancellor. The first signs of a plot against her can be seen in the arrest of Anne Askew, an evangelist with links to Catherine's ladies and to the queen herself. By spring 1546, Catherine's enemies were ready to strike.

Henry was in increasingly ill health and, by early 1546, his sixth wife had got into the habit of visiting him in his chamber, entering into religious debates with him. According to the sixteenth-century Protestant writer John Foxe, one day, as Catherine left the room, Henry remarked, 'A good hearing it is, when women become such clerks; and a thing much to my comfort, to come in mine old days to be taught by my wife.' The Bishop of Winchester, who was present, used this opportunity to persuade his master to order the queen's arrest on a charge of heresy and a warrant was drawn up. Catherine was oblivious to this and continued to debate with her husband. Shortly before the arrest was scheduled, Henry confided in his doctor, Dr Wendy, that he 'intended not any longer to be troubled with such a doctress as she was', before swearing the physician to secrecy. The arrest warrant was then found on the floor by a member of Catherine's household who brought it to the horrified queen. With the precedent of Anne Boleyn and Catherine Howard before her, Catherine became hysterical, loudly bewailing her fate. Henry heard this and sent Dr Wendy to her who, taking pity on the distressed woman, gave her the full details of the plot. It was the opportunity she needed to save herself.

The next evening, having composed herself, Catherine went to visit Henry in his bedchamber. She found her husband talking to a group of gentlemen and, when she entered, he asked her to clear up a point of doubt he had over the correct interpretation of the scriptures. Recognising this for the trap it was, Catherine responded by saying:

'Your Majesty', quoth she, 'doth right-well know, neither I myself am ignorant, what great imperfection and weakness by our first creation is allotted unto us women to be ordained and appointed as inferior and subject unto man as our head; from which head all our direction ought to proceed: and that as God made man to his own shape and likeness, whereby he, being endued with more special gifts of perfection, might rather be stirred to the contemplation of heavenly things, and to the earnest endeavour to obey his commandments, even so, also, made he woman of man, of whom and by whom she is to be governed, commanded, and directed; whose womanly weaknesses and natural imperfection ought to be tolerated, aided, and borne withal, so that, by his wisdom, such things as be lacking in her ought to be supplied.

'Since, therefore, God hath appointed such a natural difference between man and woman, and your majesty being so excellent in gifts and ornaments of wisdom, and I a silly poor woman, so much inferior in all respects of nature unto you, how then cometh it now to pass that your majesty, in such diffuse causes of religion, will seem to require my judgment? Which when I have uttered and said what I can, yet must I, and will I, refer my judgment in this, and in all other cases, to your majesty's wisdom, as my only anchor, supreme head and governor here in earth, next under God, to lean unto.'

Henry continued to press Catherine, but she was adamant, declaring that she had only disputed with him to take his mind off his illness and learn from him. With that answer, the king was entirely satisfied, saying, 'And is it even so, sweet heart!, and tended your arguments to no worse end? Then, perfect friends we are now again, as ever at any time heretofore.' He then kissed and embraced her. The couple were walking in the gardens the following day when Wriothesley came to arrest Catherine with a party of armed guards. Henry furiously turned on him, abusing him as a knave as the chancellor scurried away.

There are too many coincidences and strokes of good fortune for the plot against Catherine to be taken entirely at face value and it seems likely that Henry had meant all along to bring about her submission rather than to actively rid himself of her. In spite of this, the danger was real and Catherine was expected to change her conduct to ensure her survival. She was chastened and confined herself to a domestic sphere for the remainder of Henry's life, breathing a sigh of relief at his death on 28 January 1547.

Henry's death left Catherine free to return to her true love, Thomas Seymour. She retired with Elizabeth to her dower house at Chelsea but was soon receiving secret visits from her suitor, the uncle of the new king, Edward VI. Unbeknown to the queen, Seymour had already considered more advantageous marriages to either Princess Mary or Princess Elizabeth, but had been rejected. The dowager queen was the next best match, since he was anxious to increase his prestige with a royal marriage. He may also have retained some feelings for her. Catherine was certainly deeply in love, as one letter to Seymour shows:

I send you my most humble and hearty commendations, being desirous to know how you have done since I saw you. I pray you be not offended with me, in that I send sooner to you than I said I would, for my promise was but once in a fortnight. Howbeit the time is well abbreviated, by what means I know not, except weeks be shorter at Chelsea than in other places.

In spite of her doubts about the propriety of the marriage, she could not resist and the couple had married in secret by the end of May 1548.

Once the marriage had been celebrated, Catherine and Seymour were faced with the difficulty of publicising it. Seymour wrote to Princess Mary, asking for her support but was nonplussed when she wrote condemning any plan for the queen to remarry so soon. He next approached the young king, who was fond of both his uncle and stepmother. To their relief, the boy wrote to Catherine on 25 June giving his blessing. Seymour's brother, Edward Seymour, Duke of Somerset, who was the king's Lord Protector, took the news less favourably but, with royal consent, there was little he could do. Catherine and Seymour made their marriage public, setting up home with Princess Elizabeth and Seymour's ward, Lady Jane Grey.

While marriage to Seymour was Catherine's greatest desire, it did not bring her happiness. The Lord Protector's wife, Anne Stanhope, angered by the queen's marriage to her husband's younger brother, considered that it reduced Catherine's status. When Catherine was at court the duchess vied with her for precedence, physically pushing her aside to pass through a doorway first in the place of honour. The Duke of Somerset showed his disapproval of the match by confiscating the queen's jewels – including the wedding ring that she had received from Henry VIII. Faced with these slights, Catherine spent less time at court, retreating to her household and focussing on the upbringing and education of her two charges, Elizabeth and Jane.

Unbeknownst to Catherine, Thomas Seymour had proposed marriage to Elizabeth early in 1547. He and the girl had a mutual attraction to each other, carrying out a flirtation in the queen's household. To the scandal of Elizabeth's governess, Katherine Ashley, Seymour took to coming into the princess's bedchamber early in the morning, barelegged and in his nightclothes. If he found Elizabeth already up, he would ask 'how she did, and strike her upon the back and buttocks familiarly'. If she was still in bed, he would pull open the curtains, making as though he would enter the bed with her as she shrank back into the cushions. Sometimes he went so far as to climb up onto the mattress beside his wife's stepdaughter, tickling her playfully. This was shocking behaviour but Catherine, when she was informed of her husband's conduct, believed it to be innocent, even participating in some of the romps herself. On one occasion, in the gardens at Hanworth, the queen held Elizabeth while Seymour slashed the girl's gown into pieces.

As time went on, Catherine did begin to see that the relationship between her husband and her stepdaughter was unhealthy. On one occasion, she rebuked Mrs Ashley after claiming to have seen Elizabeth embrace a man through the gallery window. Elizabeth's governess believed that the queen invented this in order to make her keep a better watch on her charge, but Seymour and Elizabeth still had ways to meet. Finally, when Catherine found the couple embracing, she sent her stepdaughter away. The queen must have been furious with both Seymour and Elizabeth, but she parted with her stepdaughter on good terms. As Elizabeth herself recalled, at their final meeting Catherine assured her of her

The chapel royal of St George within Windsor Castle. It was in St George's that Henry chose to be interred, rather than in the Lady Chapel at Westminster Abbey that his father had built and where his parents were buried. (Elizabeth Norton)

friendship, promising that she 'would warn me of all evils that you should hear of me'.

Catherine and Elizabeth's parting in May 1548 was to be their last meeting. After three childless marriages, Catherine had surprised everyone by announcing her pregnancy early in 1548. She was already in her late thirties and suffered from ill health as she awaited the birth, but it must also have seemed miraculous. The shared anticipation of the arrival of their 'little knave' effected something of a reconciliation between husband and wife, with the couple travelling together to Sudeley Castle in Gloucestershire that summer. On 30 August 1548 Catherine gave birth to a daughter, but her health rapidly deteriorated. In her delirium she accused Seymour of wanting her dead, perhaps referring to his relationship with Elizabeth. She died on 5 September 1548 of puerperal fever.

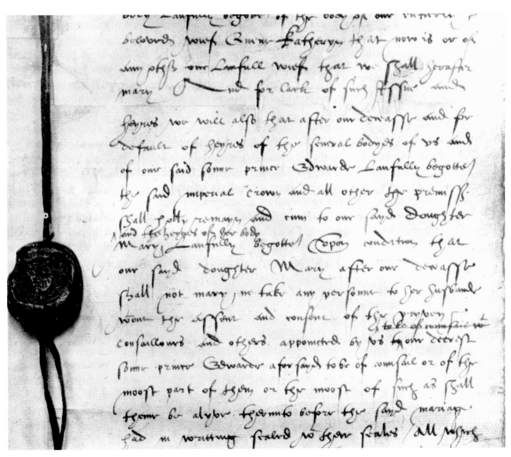

Section of Henry VIII's will, 30 December 1546, bequeathing the 'imperial crown' of England to Mary in the event of Edward's death without issue. While Edward is described as Henry's 'deerest sonne prince Edward', Mary is simply his 'daughter'. (Jonathan Reeve, JRCD2b20p961 15501600)

Following Catherine's death, Seymour, who had for months been plotting against his brother, became increasingly unstable. After an attempt to abduct the king early in 1549, he was executed for treason. Catherine's daughter, Mary Seymour, who was left a penniless orphan, disappeared from the records in her infancy, suggesting that she did not long survive her parents.

* * *

The six wives of Henry VIII lived varied lives and had differing fortunes. The lives of all six were blighted by the terrifying king and his attempts to secure the succession of a male heir. When Catherine Parr was offered the dubious honour of becoming Henry's sixth wife, she reportedly said that it was better to be his mistress. This, on the whole, was true, with most of Henry VIII's mistresses going on to lead contended lives once they had been discarded by the king.

Catherine Parr from her tomb at Sudeley Castle. (Elizabeth Norton)

Lady Jane Grey. (Elizabeth Norton)

An Allegory of the Tudor Succession. Painted in the reign of Elizabeth to celebrate the harmony established during her reign, it shows Henry VIII on his throne, passing the sword of justice to his son Edward VI. On the left are Mary I and her husband, Philip II of Spain, with Mars, the God of War. On the right, Elizabeth holds the hand of Peace with Plenty following behind. (Yale Centre for British Art, Paul Mellon Collection)

Henry VIII, Edward VI, Mary I and Elizabeth I. Hendrick Goltzius, 1584. (Rijksmuseum)

7

The Mistresses of Henry VIII

Henry VIII's six wives were not the only women to share his bed during his long reign. Although far from the lecherous figure of popular imagination, Henry did take a number of mistresses, some of whom are well known today.

As a prince, Henry was kept strictly ('locked away like a woman') by his over-protective father. As king, however, he was free to indulge himself in extra-marital affairs, particularly since, in his youth, he was reputed to be one of the most handsome men in Europe. The first woman to whom his name was linked was Anne Stafford, in 1510. Anne, who was married, served the queen alongside her sister Elizabeth. There was apparently some jealousy between the sisters, since Elizabeth informed their brother, the Duke of Buckingham, that Anne was 'suspected with the king', causing the peer to storm into her apartments to remonstrate with her. Henry, on hearing of this, reprimanded the duke, with Buckingham leaving court for a time. It was also the end of the affair since Anne's husband, Lord Hastings, removed her to a convent, while Catherine of Aragon, who would later learn to ignore Henry's infidelities, appeared 'vexed' with him in public. The affair was a short one and played out embarrassingly publicly. The king's subsequent affairs were usually more discrete.

Anne Stafford may have been succeeded in the king's affections by Etienne de la Baume, whom Henry met in 1513 during his military campaign in France. Etienne, who was an attendant of Margaret of Austria, Regent of the Netherlands, later wrote to the English king to claim a promised dowry of 10,000 crowns. Such an enormous sum is an indication that the couple were romantically involved, with Etienne reminding Henry that, during their meeting, 'you spoke many pretty things to me'. Another Frenchwoman, Jane Popincourt, who was resident at the English court, was also rumoured to be his mistress. She was older than Henry and served his sister Mary Tudor as a lady in waiting. When she returned permanently to France in 1516, she took a gift of £100 from the English king, later becoming the lover of the Duke of Longueville.

Another rumoured early mistress was Elizabeth Boleyn, who was some years older than the king and the mother of his second wife, Anne. In 1533 a Mistress Amadas, who was the wife of a goldsmith and connected by marriage to Bessie Blount, found herself in trouble when she declared that 'my lady Anne [Boleyn] should be burned, for she is a harlot; that Master Norris was bawd between the king and her; that the king kept both the mother and daughter, and that my lord of Wiltshire [Elizabeth's husband, Thomas] was bawd both to his wife and his two daughters'. There were evidently contemporary rumours that Elizabeth had shared the king's bed, with the Jesuit Nicholas Sander claiming late in the sixteenth century that Anne Boleyn was actually Henry VIII's illegitimate daughter. In spite of these claims, it seems unlikely that Elizabeth ever served as a roal mistress, since Henry VIII himself denied it. When, in 1529, Sir George Throckmorton attempted to dissuade the king from marrying Anne, he pointed out that 'it is thought you have meddled both with the mother and sister', something to which Henry responded, 'Never with the mother.' He could not make the same denial regarding Anne's sister, Mary Boleyn.

In October 1514, Henry's friend Charles Brandon, Duke of Suffolk, concluded a letter to the king saying, 'I beseech your Grace to [tell] Mistress Blount and Mistress Carew the next time that I write unto them or send them tokens they shall either write to me or send me tokens again.' This is the first indication that Henry had noticed a young maid of his wife's, Bessie Blount, who was aged around fifteen or sixteen and came from a Shropshire gentry family. At first, however, his attention appears to have been focussed on Elizabeth Carew, who also served the queen and was the sister of Henry's friend, Sir Francis Bryan. Earlier that year Elizabeth had married the courtier Nicholas Carew and both soon began to receive lavish gifts from the king. In Henry's wardrobe accounts from 1516, for example, Nicholas Carew received fine gifts of clothing, including a purple mantle augmented with black fur and a crimson velvet gown with a stylish high collar. His wife received even finer gifts, particularly favouring cloth of silver. Henry also gave her the intimate gift of a 'stomacher', which was an item of clothing designed to be worn close to the body. The gifts to Elizabeth in these accounts, which were far beyond anything received by the other court ladies, strongly hints at an affair between the king and Elizabeth Carew. On one occasion he appears to have made gifts of the same silver damask cloth to his wife and his mistress. Long after the affair had ended, when Elizabeth had fallen on hard times, she pointedly wrote to the king's chief minister to remind him that 'all that I have had in my life hath been of his grace, and I trust that his grace will not see me lack'.

The beautiful Elizabeth, or Bessie, Blount soon superseded Elizabeth Carew in the king's affections. At New Year 1515 Henry danced with her during the revels. Later that year he also made a generous payment to Bessie's father, John Blount, who was a member of his bodyguard (the King's Spears), paying him two years' wages in advance at a time when he was considering disbanding John's unit. John was also appointed as one of the king's esquires of the body in 1517, although he did not receive a knighthood until 1529. Bessie Blount was well educated, possessing works of English literature, such as John Gower's *Confessio Amantis* and Chaucer's *Troilus and Criseyde*. It is uncertain when, exactly, the affair began, although Bessie made her last public appearance at court in October 1518, when she was already in the early stages of pregnancy. On 10 November

Bessie Blount from the side of her parents' tomb.
(Elizabeth Norton)

1518 Catherine of Aragon gave birth to a stillborn daughter as a tragic end to what would prove to be her last pregnancy. In light of this Bessie, who would around that period have been required to add a panel to the front of her gown ('as ladies in the family-way are wont to do in this country, when they find their robes get too tight'), was sent away. Henry arranged for her to stay in the prior's house in the Priory of St Lawrence at Blackmore in Essex – a residence that was easily accessible from London. It was there, probably on 18 June 1519, that Bessie gave birth to a son. Henry VIII admitted paternity immediately, causing the child to be named Henry Fitzroy (with the surname translating as 'illegitimate son of the king'), while sending Cardinal Wolsey to stand as godfather. After the birth Bessie Blount did not return to court, although she is likely to have received visits that summer from the king who was staying nearby in Essex. By the end of the summer she was pregnant again, bearing a daughter, Elizabeth, at some point between April and June 1520. This daughter was acknowledged by Gilbert Tailboys, a young nobleman in the service of Cardinal Wolsey, who was selected to marry the king's cast-off mistress. However, the fact that there is no record that the couple were married before March 1522 strongly suggests that Elizabeth was, in fact, also the child of the king.

Bessie Blount and Gilbert Tailboys received a number of financial grants from the king, while Gilbert was also ennobled as Lord Tailboys. Bessie probably spent much of her marriage in Lincolnshire, where she bore at least two further sons.

Henry Fitzroy. Bessie's
eldest son bore a
strong resemblance
to his royal father,
who delighted in him.
(Elizabeth Norton)

She was also free to visit court, as well as her eldest son, Henry Fitzroy. The boy, who was cherished by his father, was ennobled as Duke of Richmond and Somerset in June 1525 and sent to nominally rule the north of the kingdom. As a widow, attention briefly focussed on Bessie once more when there were rumours that Henry meant to divorce Catherine of Aragon and marry her. However, nothing came of this and the former mistress instead married a young man named Edward Clinton. She bore three further daughters before dying, probably in 1539, three years after the death of her eldest son.

Bessie Blount was replaced as the king's mistress by Mary Boleyn, who was a similar age to her and had received some education in France. She appears to have returned to the English court in 1514 under something of a cloud, amid rumours that she had become the mistress of Francis I of France. Certainly, the ungallant Francis, who called Henry VIII's sister Mary Tudor, 'more dirty than queenly', had something to say about Mary Boleyn in later years, declaring that she was 'a very great whore and infamous above all'. Her reputation was not completely lost, however, since she had secured a place with Catherine of Aragon by at least 1520. Earlier that year she had also married William Carey, a young gentleman who was a favourite with the king.

At that time Bessie Blount was awaiting the birth of her second child, something which gave Mary the opportunity to replace her as royal mistress. Her husband's acceptance was bought with a number of royal grants, including the keepership of New Hall in Essex – the fine palace that the king had used as his base when

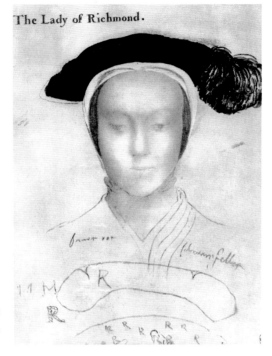

The Lady of Richmond.

Right: Mary Howard, daughter of Thomas Howard, 3rd Duke of Norfolk, who was married in 1533 to Henry Fitzroy, Duke of Richmond, Henry VIII's acknowledged bastard son. (Stephen Porter)

Below: The tomb of Henry Fitzroy at St Michael's church, Framlingham, Suffolk. (Elizabeth Norton)

he visited Bessie Blount at Blackmoor. During this period, Mary also bore two children: Catherine and Henry Carey. Henry, the younger of the two, is known to have been born on 4 March 1526, while Catherine was born in around 1524. There were certainly rumours that the children were Henry's, with the vicar of Isleworth recalling in April 1535 that 'Mr Skidmore did show to me young Master Carey, saying that he was our sovereign lord the king's son by our sovereign lady the queen's [Anne Boleyn's] sister, whom the queen's grace might not suffer to be in the court'. Both children may plausibly be Henry VIII's, although the fact that Mary was married must make any identity of their paternity a cautious one, particularly since they were never acknowledged. Catherine, who was born earlier in the relationship, is more likely to be Henry's child than Henry Carey, since William Carey was evidently content that this child was his heir.

William Carey died suddenly of the sweating sickness in 1528, leaving Mary a widow. Her affair with the king was long since over and she may have been directly supplanted by her sister in 1527. As Anne Boleyn's sister, Mary continued to have a place at court, serving her sister when she became queen. She caused a scandal in the summer of 1534 when she arrived at court, obviously pregnant. It soon emerged that she had married a servant, William Stafford, when 'love

Mary Boleyn.
(Hever Castle)

overcame reason' between them. It appears to have been a true love match, since Mary would later write that 'for my part I saw so much honesty in him, that I loved him as well as he did me, and was in bondage and glad I was to be at liberty: so that, for my part, I saw that all the world did set so little by me, and he so much, that I thought I could take no better way but to take him and to forsake all other ways, and live a poor, honest life with him'. When the match was discovered, Mary was sent away by her furious sister and parents, but she was unrepentant, writing that 'if I were at my liberty and might choose, I ensure you, master secretary, for my little time, I have tried so much honesty to be in him, that I had rather beg my bread with him than be the greatest queen in Christendom'. She had reconciled with her sister by early 1536. It must have been bitter when she heard her name mentioned – in connection with her affair with the king – as a means of annulling her sister's marriage. With the executions of her brother and sister, Mary was her father's sole heir, inheriting his property after his death in 1539. She died on 19 July 1543.

Mary Boleyn was not the only relative of Anne Boleyn's to share the king's bed. During his marriage, Henry was regularly unfaithful. An unknown woman, known as the 'Imperial Lady' caused trouble in 1534. She used her royal influence to aid Catherine of Aragon and Princess Mary, causing Anne and her sister-in-law, Lady Rochford, to plot her downfall. She was supplanted by Anne's own cousin 'Madge' Shelton in February 1535. This 'Madge' has not been identified with certainty, since she may be either Margaret Shelton or her younger sister, Mary, both of whom were daughters of Sir John Shelton and his wife, Anne, who was the sister of Anne Boleyn's father, Sir Thomas Boleyn. Margaret, who married Thomas Wodehouse of Kimberley in Norfolk, is not known to have had a court post, while her sister was regularly noted there. It is therefore more likely that 'Madge' was the beautiful and highly intelligent Mary Shelton. Although Mary managed to supplant the Imperial Lady, who had caused Anne so much trouble, the queen was far from happy with her cousin taking a place in Henry's affections. When Anne found her idly writing verses in her prayer book one day she took the opportunity to publicly rebuke her for such 'wanton toys', before commanding 'the mother of maidens to have a more vigilant eye to her charge'. Given that Anne herself had once exchanged such verses in her prayer book with Henry, it seems more likely that this incident was an excuse to display her authority to her young cousin, as well as to ensure that she was kept under close observation. The affair was not, in any event, long lasting, although it may have been the cause of the breach between Anne and her aunt Lady Shelton, whom she would later refer to as a woman 'she had never loved'.

Mary Shelton remained at court for some years after her cousin's fall, attracting the attention of the poet, Sir Thomas Wyatt, who wrote verse expressing his love for her. She had also attracted the attention of the newlywed Francis Weston by the time of his arrest for adultery with Anne, who spoke to the young man of the fact that 'he did love her kinswoman Mrs Shelton'. She may also have been the

If the label is correct, then this is a painting of 'Madge' Shelton, believed to be Mary Shelton, first cousin to Anne Boleyn. (Stephen Porter)

'Madge' who was loved by Henry Norris, who also died with Anne Boleyn. Mary Shelton often found herself involved in love affairs. In the 1540s she fell in love with her cousin Thomas Clere, who was a well-liked young man at court. Mary moved in literary circles, and was a friend of Henry Howard, Earl of Surrey. She composed her own poetry, which survives in a remarkable manuscript known as the Devonshire Manuscript (held by the British Library). In one poem she declared that she was unable to 'make a joke of all my woe', since she was forced 'to cloak my grief where it doth grow'. She also gave her works a remarkably feminist slant, in one case, when transcribing Chaucer, changing a line from 'the cursedness yet and deceit of women' to read 'the faithfulness yet and praise of women'. Mary's writings in the Devonshire Manuscript made it clear that she had been part of a scandal and that she considered herself to have been wronged by one particular man, although whether this was Norris, Weston, Wyatt, Clere or even Henry VIII, it is not clear. After Clere's early death in 1545, Mary finally settled down, marrying Sir Anthony Heveningham. She bore several children, as well as marrying once more, soon after her husband's death in 1557. She died in 1560 in her early forties.

Although Mary Shelton's brief affair with Henry VIII was over in 1536, she caught his eye once again in 1538, following the death of Jane Seymour. On 3 January 1538 John Husee, the London agent of Lord Lisle, wrote to inform his master that 'the election lieth betwixt Mrs Mary Shelton and Mrs Mary Skipwith. I pray Jesu send such one as may be for his Highness' comfort and the wealth of the realm', before cautioning his master to keep silent on the matter. The letter suggests that Henry was considering an affair, or perhaps even a marriage, to one of the two ladies. If so, his choice appears to have fallen on Mistress Skipwith. As with Mary Shelton, there were two sisters who can potentially be identified as the object of Henry's affections: Mary and Margaret. They were the daughters of Sir William Skipwith of Ormsby – a solid Lincolnshire gentleman. There is no evidence that Mary, who was soon to marry, ever attended court, and Margaret Skipwith is the more likely candidate. She was young when she attracted the king's attention, and the affair was very soon over. Conveniently, Henry was able to find a husband for her in young George Tailboys, the teenaged son of Bessie Blount, as well as later paying her dowry when she took a second husband.

Henry VIII squeezed his last five marriages into the final fourteen years of his life and this, coupled with the fact that he tended to marry Englishwomen who caught his eye, meant that he had few known mistresses in this period. He retained a roving eye right up to the end of his life, with Catherine Willoughby, the Dowager Duchess of Suffolk rumoured to be a potential seventh wife as the king began to tire of Catherine Parr. In February 1546, the Imperial ambassador, Van der Delft, reported

Catherine Willoughby became the fourth wife of Charles Brandon, Duke of Suffolk, in 1535, at the tender age of fourteen. Had Henry lived a few months longer, she might have become his seventh queen. (Elizabeth Norton)

that there were already rumours of a new queen and that 'Madame Suffolk is much talked about and is in great favour', a rumour that 'annoyed' the queen. Catherine Willoughby, who was the widow of Charles Brandon, Duke of Suffolk, and a great heiress in her own right, was the intellectual equal of Catherine Parr and shared her interest in religious reform. There is no evidence that she ever served as Henry's mistress, but she seems to have attracted him. He died refusing to see his wife, only a few short months after he had planned her arrest. Who knows, if Henry VIII had lived a few months longer history might recall the seven wives of Henry VIII, with Catherine Willoughby the last of that number and the survivor of them all?

***

'Divorced, beheaded, died, divorced, beheaded, survived' does not do justice to the lives of the six women who dared to marry Henry VIII, nor the lives of the other women who shared his bed, and their stories are still engaging and fascinating today.

Further Reading

The six wives of Henry VIII have always been a popular subject for historians. A number of general books exist, such as Hume, M., *The Wives of Henry VIII*; Fraser, A., *The Six Wives of Henry VIII* (1992); Weir, A., *The Six Wives of Henry VIII* (2007); Starkey, D., *Six Wives* (2003); and Loades, D., *The Six Wives of Henry VIII* (2009). Mackay, L., *Inside the Tudor Court* (2014), which tells the story of Eustace Chapuys, the Imperial ambassador to England, also provides fascinating detail on Henry's queens.

All of the six wives have also now been the subject of at least one biography. For **Catherine of Aragon**, Mattingly, G., *Catherine of Aragon* (1944) is excellent, although dated in places. Tremlett, G., *Catherine of Aragon* (2010) is more recent and makes interesting use of Spanish sources. Fox, J., *Sister Queens* (2011) and Williams, P., *Katharine of Aragon* (2013) are also recent. Older biographies include Luke, M. M., *Catherine the Queen* (1967) and Paul, J. E., *Catherine of Aragon and Her Friends*.

Anne Boleyn has been the subject of a wealth of biographies. The most detailed is Ives, E. W., *The Life and Death of Anne Boleyn* (Oxford, 2005). Others include Bengar, E. O., *Memoirs of the Life of Anne Boleyn*, 2 vols (1821); Bernard, G. W., *Anne Boleyn: Fatal Attractions* (2010); Bruce, M. L., *Anne Boleyn* (1972); Chapman, H. W., *Anne Boleyn* (1974); Denny, J., *Anne Boleyn* (2004); Erickson, C., *Anne Boleyn* (1984); Friedmann, P., *Anne Boleyn* (1884); Norton, E., *Anne Boleyn: Henry VIII's Obsession* (2008); and Sergeant, P. W., *The Life of Anne Boleyn* (1923). Other works focus on specific periods of Anne's life, such as Weir, A., *The Lady in the Tower* (2009) and Wilkinson, J., *The Early Loves of Anne Boleyn* (2009).

Jane Seymour has never attracted as much attention as her two predecessors. However, she is the subject of three books: Gross, P., *Jane the Quene* (1999); Loades, D., *Jane Seymour* (2012); and Norton, E., *Jane Seymour: Henry VIII's True Love* (2009). You can also read more about her family in Seymour, W., *Ordeal by Ambition* (1972).

Anne of Cleves is the subject of two biographies: Norton, E., *Anne of Cleves: Henry VIII's Discarded Bride* (2009) and Saaler, A., *Anne of Cleves* (1997). Warnicke, R.M., *The Marrying of Anne of Cleves* (2000) presents a scholarly account of her marriage.

For **Catherine Howard,** the most detailed work has been carried out by Lacey Baldwin Smith. His biography of Catherine was recently reissued as *Catherine Howard* (2008). Denny, J., *Katherine Howard* (2005) and Loades, D., *Catherine Howard* (2013) are also biographies.

Catherine Parr has been the subject of four recent biographies: James, S., *Catherine Parr* (2008); Norton, E., *Catherine Parr* (2010); Porter, L., *Katherine the Queen* (2010); and Withrow, B. G., *Katherine Parr* (2009). An older biography, which is still useful, is Martienssen, A., *Queen Katherine Parr* (1975).

For the **mistresses,** try Norton, E., *Bessie Blount* (2011), which is a comprehensive biography of Henry VIII's most important mistress. There are also two biographies of Mary Boleyn: Weir, A., *Mary Boleyn* (2011) and Wilkinson, J., *Mary Boleyn* (2009). Hart, K., *Mistresses of Henry VIII* (2010) gives detail about these and other lovers of Henry VIII. Norton, E., *The Boleyn Women* (2013) looks in detail at Henry's relationships with Elizabeth Boleyn, Mary Boleyn and 'Madge' Shelton.

It is also easy to access primary source material for the six wives. Norton, E. (ed.), *The Anne Boleyn Papers* (2013) collects together many of the leading sources for Anne, including her correspondence, Henry VIII's love letters, the dispatches of Eustace Chapuys and extracts from chronicles and other sixteenth-century sources. This book was previously published as *Anne Boleyn in Her Own Words and the Words of Those Who Knew Her* (2011). Other important sources include Cavendish, G., *Thomas Wolsey Late Cardinal: His Life and Death*, Lockyer, R. (ed.) (1962); Hall, E., *Chronicle Containing the History of England*; Johnson, J., et al (eds) (1809); St Clare Byrne, M. (ed.), *The Lisle Letters*, 6 vols (1981); Strype, J., *Ecclesiastical Memorials* (1822); and Wriothesley, C., *A Chronicle of England During the Reigns of the Tudors*, 2 vols, Hamilton, W.D. (ed.) (1875–8). Many of the nineteenth-century books are available to view on the internet at sites such as www.archive.org.